CLIMATE CRISIS

THE CHALLENGE TO THE CHURCH

DAVID RHODES

kevin
mayhew

First published in Great Britain in 2020 by Kevin Mayhew Ltd,
Buxhall, Stowmarket, Suffolk IP14 3BW
Tel: +44 (0) 1449 737978 Fax: +44 (0) 1449 737834
E-mail: info@kevinmayhew.com

www.kevinmayhew.com

9 8 7 6 5 4 3 2 1 0

ISBN 978 1 83858 081 0
Catalogue No. 1501666

Cover design by Rob Mortonson
© Images used under licence from Shutterstock
Edited by Linda Ottewell
Typeset by Rob Mortonson

Printed and bound in Great Britain

Contents

About the Author

As an Anglican priest, David Rhodes worked for many years alongside vulnerable and homeless people in Leeds. His best-selling books on faith and social justice were inspired by those encounters, leading to his innovative 'retreats on the streets' and his nationally recognised One City urban theology project. He is a former director of the Bible Reading Fellowship, chaplain to the Children's Society and member of General Synod. His first book, *Faith in Dark Places,* led to him presenting a Good Friday meditation on urban spirituality on BBC1 and other television appearances. Before ordination, David worked as a journalist. More recently he has written on prayer and social justice for the Iona Community, the Church Urban Fund, Church Action on Poverty and the Industrial Christian Fellowship.

In Praise of *Climate Crisis*

'A powerful reminder that the gospel is a subversive message that challenges oppression and calls us to be on the side of the marginalised.'
Church Action on Poverty

'Rates among the great theological texts of our time – alongside Jenkins and Spong. Full of fresh insights and connections. Awesome, inspiring, brilliant . . .'
Nigel Greenwood, *Former chair, Ripon Diocesan Board of Education and Director, One City Projects*

'Great theology. I loved it!'
Dr Helen Reid, *Director, Leeds Church Institute*

'An important book and a terrific read.'
Warren Bardsley, *the Iona Community*

Introduction:
The fourth denial

The world is in serious trouble. The lives of millions of people are blighted by poverty, injustice and racism. But, overshadowing all this, the emerging crisis of climate change is rapidly destroying God's creation and threatening our survival as a species. Our poorest neighbours are already suffering acutely but it will be our children and their children, who will bear the full impact of the disaster.

By inspiring its two billion members to action, the worldwide Church could play a pivotal role in averting this looming catastrophe. Instead it agonises over its own survival and worries about who is sleeping with whom.

The reason for this disastrous introversion is that the Church has distorted the Jesus vision of radical social justice, summed up in the call to love our neighbour. It has buried him under a mountain of religion, blinding us to his message of love and liberation. Peter denied Christ three times after Jesus was arrested but the Church is guilty of a far greater fourth denial by its conspiracy of silence.

The enormity of the threat of climate change means re-engagement with the real Jesus of the Gospels is imperative. But for this to happen, it is necessary to strip away some basic theological assumptions blocking that process. To play its essential part in halting global warming, the Church needs to recalibrate its understanding of why it exists – and to do so urgently. This may sound an impossible task but the process is essential if vested interests and institutional inertia are to be overcome and catastrophe averted.

That is the challenge explored in this book. The outcome hangs in the balance.

1

In the beginning…

In the beginning was the Onion. Or at least at the beginning of the Jesus story, there was the Onion. The Church never tells you about the Onion, and it's important to ask why it keeps that information to itself.

Often when I go to the supermarket, I notice that the onions in the fruit and vegetable section are always perfectly round: not at all like the sort I grow in my allotment. My home-grown onions always look a bit squashed. But, oddly enough, it's my slightly squashed onions with their long, thin stalks that are exactly the shape of the Jesus Onion.

Why does this matter? Because our understanding of the Onion is vital to our understanding of Jesus: what he did and said. In fact it raises alarming questions about much that the Church has been doing over the last two thousand years.

It happened this way: not long ago, researchers investigated what was going on in first-century Palestine. In particular they asked how that ancient society was structured in terms of wealth, power and status. Who were the big winners and who were the losers? They discovered that the mass of the population lived in poverty, while a tiny ruling elite controlled vast wealth and influence – and made very sure they hung on to what they'd got.

Helpfully, the researchers drew a diagram of the situation. I don't think they had onions in mind when they drew it, but when I saw the diagram, I realised it was roughly the shape of one of my squashed onions. It looked a bit like this:

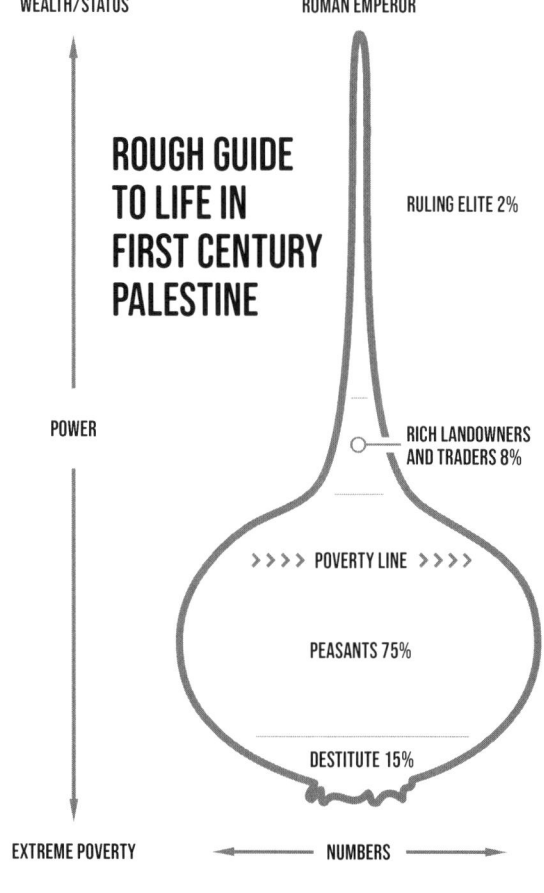

The vertical axis of the diagram indicates power, wealth and status and the horizontal axis the number of people. The poverty line is approximate.

First-century Palestine was occupied and ruled by the Romans. So, not surprisingly, at the very tip of the onion stalk with enormous status and power is the emperor, Caesar. Below him in power and status are a small number of other extremely rich and powerful people. As we come down the long, thin stalk, you realise that massive wealth is held by a tiny elite – as in the world today.

It is only at much lower levels of wealth and power that the diagram begins to open out into the bulb of the Onion, representing about 90 per cent of the population. Right down in the bottom 15 per cent of the onion bulb is a group of people so poor and lacking in status that they were hardly recognised as being human. Where exactly the poverty line came is not clear but it was probably well up in the onion bulb. This would suggest that most people in first-century Palestine experienced real poverty. Many struggled to survive in absolute destitution. And they were far from happy.

I must confess all this came as a surprise to me. I had always assumed that Jesus lived in an essentially calm and stable society. The picture of Jesus I saw at Sunday School was of a white man with fair hair and well-laundered robes going about doing kind things. I assumed that what poverty there might have been arose because of illness or personal misfortune, as in the story of the widow's mite, but that most people were comfortably off.

So the Day of the Onion came as something of a shock. It changed my view of Jesus and the Church. And it changed me. I switched from my passive, kindly ordained clergy mode to that of my previous existence as a national newspaper journalist.

The poverty gap

One of the great things about being a journalist is that you are allowed to be ignorant. Your job is to ask questions, not to know the answers. Sometimes your questions might appear simplistic but it's only by asking questions that a journalist gets the story. And to get the real story you may need to ask some very awkward questions.

The first questions I asked were: why the Onion? Why is it that shape? Why are Caesar and the political elite so much richer and more powerful than the people at the bottom of the onion bulb?

Obviously life is easier if you have power and wealth and it's nice if people look up to you. It gives you a sense of worth and significance. But that only works when your power and wealth are greater than other people's. And that difference is important. If everyone has equal wealth and power, then nobody is going to be willing to perform the menial and unpleasant tasks in life. The rich and powerful can only enjoy power and status when other people are denied power and status. For one group to be rich, another group needs to be less rich. In other words, the rich need the poor to be poor. Apart from anything else it gives them a large pool of cheap labour.

The vast social distance between the rich and poor also gives the rich a feeling of security. A sense of their own importance. So when someone asks:

'What meaning does your life have?' the rich can answer: 'I have achieved power, wealth, possessions and status. All that gives meaning to my life.'

A second question follows on from this: how do the rich stay rich? The answer is that they take from the people below them by multiple forms of taxation and the frequent confiscation of land. But the people below them do not willingly part with their money and produce, so they have to be forced to do so.

To make this process of extraction operate more smoothly, and to counter the inevitable protests from the people, the rich and powerful argue they deserve their money and possessions by way of recompense for maintaining peace in civil society.

The *Pax Romana*, the Peace of Rome, which was imposed across the empire, sounded a brilliant idea – but it was a peace imposed and maintained at the point of the sword. Behind that so-called peace was the constant threat of terror. It was a high-class protection racket. The historian Tacitus knew exactly what was going on and pilloried the Romans for being 'robbers of the world, insatiable for domination and profit'.

Not only were the rich and powerful able to extract wealth and services from those below them, but they increasingly came to believe that they were entitled to do so. Perhaps even that God, or the gods, had put them in this position. That it was divinely ordained that they, and not others, should have power and status.

This raises the question of the selective way in which religion has been used to legitimise privilege and power.

For example, how is it that a monarch is traditionally anointed by a priest at his or her coronation but the people who empty our rubbish bins are not? These days monarchy wields far less direct power than in the past, but as the pinnacle of a system of status, privilege and inequality it helps to legitimise structural injustice.

The third question that arose in first-century Palestine was: why do the rich need to be so very rich? Why are they so greedy? One answer is that wealth and power work like a drug. The more people have, the more most of them seem to crave. But, if that is so, then we are not simply talking about success and social status but about the pathology of greed.

Uneasy lies the head

In the century before Jesus was born, two things happened that were to have a major impact. Firstly, the Roman Empire was getting bigger as more territory was conquered. The people doing the conquering were the Roman military, and in particular its generals. But as the empire expanded, it became much harder to govern. Instead of a vague form of democracy that had operated for centuries, a much more effective model of leadership was needed.

The result was that, around 50BCE, the democratic process was replaced by a dictatorship. The first such dictator to be appointed for life was Julius Caesar, but the new system had serious teething troubles. Julius took absolute power in the January of 44BCE. Six weeks later he was assassinated. He hardly had time to unpack his bags.

What has all this got to do with Jesus and first-century Palestine? Quite a lot. Civil war and political assassination had been around a long time in the Roman world. Rulers often had brief careers and this led to a sense of national insecurity. Then came further political change. In 9CE Augustus Caesar decreed that further military conquests should cease. As a result, the Roman army's role changed from one of heroic conquest to the control and maintenance of conquered territories. The warrior became the policeman.

But military achievement had been a major source of status and honour, so where was that status to come from now? One answer was real estate. In particular the construction of impressive and extremely expensive cities, buildings and statues. As the population and the built environment of Rome increased, the whole project became vastly more expensive. Where was the money (and the food) to come from? The conquered territories.

The vacuum cleaner

The long stalk of the Onion was now working like a vacuum cleaner hose. The extraction of produce and wealth to feed mighty Rome operated on an industrial scale. North Africa became the bread basket of the empire and Spain was turned over almost completely to the production of olive oil. The knock-on effect on the population of first-century Palestine was grim. Poverty worsened. Small farms were increasingly taken over by wealthy absentee landowners and many peasants, who had farmed their land for generations, were made homeless.

This process of exploitation was probably common to most of the territories that came under Roman rule but for the Hebrews there was a further and acute dynamic to their suffering. They believed that their land had been given to them by God, but now it was controlled and desecrated by an alien pagan power. There was a sense of corporate shame that such a thing had been allowed to happen.

Secondly, there was a bitter sense of betrayal by the Hebrew aristocracy. The Roman army was a mighty military force, but even Caesar's many legions could not control every town and village in the vast occupied territories.

The solution to the problem was that the Romans co-opted local tribal leaders into the control function. The trade off was that, in return for collusion, the indigenous leaders were rewarded with status and power. Local leaders who refused to cooperate were probably eliminated. In the case of first-century Palestine, not only the king but also the chief priest was appointed by Rome. The wealthy elite were seduced by the glamour of Rome and the privileges offered in return for cooperation.

In addition, the Temple in Jerusalem became a focus of exploitation and oppression of the people. It is tempting to assume the Temple was rather like a cathedral, but the temple complex was vast and included a number of diverse functions. As taxation and offerings poured in it became inordinately rich, operating in a way not dissimilar to a bank. Secondly, sacrifices were carried out on a massive scale with as many as 10,000 animals being slaughtered annually. Thirdly, controlled absolutely by the political elite, the Temple became the primary power centre, drawing in wealth from the impoverished rural population and operating like a vast storehouse for the benefit of the rich.

This situation sparked widespread anger and resentment. There were sporadic armed uprisings against the military occupation and the corruption of the Temple by groups called the zealots. Such rebellions were easily crushed by the Romans and usually punished by crucifixion.

It was into this nightmare that Jesus was born. Welcome to the Onion.

2

Rediscovering the real Jesus

So what happens if we lay our diagram of the Onion alongside the gospel accounts of Jesus and compare and contrast the two?

For centuries the image of Jesus presented by the Church has been that he was kind and gentle and the stories he told were, on the whole, reassuringly safe stories. He had arguments with people in authority but, we are led to believe, these were largely 'religious' and 'spiritual' disagreements. The trouble is that the onion diagram raises some very serious doubts about that. In the next few pages we are going to be taking a journalist's look at what Jesus seems to have said and at what he did.

First, the Agenda.

According to the Gospel of Luke (chapter 4, verses 16 - 21) Jesus goes to a synagogue and is invited to read from the scriptures. He finds the passage from the prophet Isaiah that says:

'The Spirit of the Lord is upon me, because he has anointed me to preach good news to the poor. He has sent me to proclaim release to the captives and recovering of sight to the blind, to set at liberty those who are oppressed, to proclaim the acceptable year of the Lord.'

After finishing the reading he sits down. But then he says something controversial: 'Today this scripture has been fulfilled in your hearing.'

At first the congregation are impressed with his gracious words but within minutes the mood changes to one of alarm and anger as they realise the words of Isaiah's agenda are about to be put into action. According to the gospel writer, Jesus narrowly escapes being killed by the crowd.

What was all that about? Why does it matter to us, two thousand years later? And what has it got to do with the Onion?

If we listen to this gospel story and then think about the onion diagram, several issues jump out at us. Jesus is saying he has been anointed by God for a purpose. First on the list is to bring good news to the poor. But who were the poor? Not just a few people who had fallen on difficult times and were only just managing to make ends meet. The poor were the mass of the population, many of them struggling to survive under a harsh political and economic regime imposed by the Romans – with the help of the Jewish religious hierarchy. But what would be good news for them?

Whether it is first-century Palestine or our twenty-first century world, good news for the poor is about food, shelter, stability, the freedom to grow into the fullness of life in a nurturing environment. It is about being shown respect and having dignity.

However, as we have already seen, the poor are kept poor by the rich, who need the poor to remain poor.

That is how people with power want things to be. Good news for the poor is therefore bad news for the rich. An idea likely to be opposed strongly and violently by those in power.

In Matthew's version of the Beatitudes (chapter 5, verse 3) we have slightly different words, with Jesus saying 'Blessed are the poor *in spirit.*' Many in the Church prefer this 'spiritualised' version and say Jesus meant people whose souls are troubled – as the souls of all believers are likely to be from time to time.

But think back again to the Onion. What was happening to the vast majority of the people? Poverty, dispossession of land, homelessness, trauma, a burning sense of injustice. A sense of impotence in the minds of parents ashamed that they could not give their children security. Perhaps powerful feelings of guilt that their generation had somehow allowed the disaster of the occupation to happen. Alarm that God seemed to have abandoned them to their fate.

Distress and confusion in the minds of children at seeing their parents dishonoured by poverty and oppression. Fear that their fathers might end up crucified as others had been for daring to challenge the occupation by joining in an uprising by the militant zealots. Dread that the soldiers might come in the night and take their fathers away.

A powerful weapon

The South African Steve Biko, who led the Black Consciousness Movement in the apartheid years, once said that the most powerful weapon in the hands of the oppressor was the mind of the oppressed.

The mind of the oppressed was also the most powerful weapon in the hands of the Romans and the indigenous tribal leaders who colluded with them. Matthew's 'poor in spirit' might have referred to people traumatised and crushed in spirit. A people robbed of hope and dignity. A people oppressed and psychologically held captive by the awesome might of Rome. Maybe St Matthew wasn't offering us a spiritual soft option, but describing a stark and brutal reality.

And what about the tag line coming along at the end of that Isaiah reading: to proclaim the year of the Lord's favour? A gentle sounding phrase but one that would ring alarm bells among the rich. It was a reference to the ancient Hebrew idea that every fifty years all debts should be cancelled and all land appropriated by the rich should be restored to its original owner.

But debt was one of the most powerful levers of control exerted by the rich on the poor. Crushing, humiliating debt. Small farmers frequently fell into debt when their crops failed. When that happened they would then have to borrow to buy food for this year and seed corn for the next. If they couldn't repay the debt on time, the creditor could take land in lieu of payment. This was a classic method of appropriating land for the rich and a major cause of poverty and destitution among the poor who were often reduced to seasonal day work – zero hours contracts.

As for many in our own world, debt in first-century Palestine was a massive burden for the poor. So how did that sound to the people listening to Jesus when he said *today* this dream of justice was beginning to come true?

Think also for a moment about the line in the Lord's Prayer when Jesus tells the crowds to pray that their trespasses might be forgiven. Trespasses sounds a very spiritual word. It conjures up thoughts about our souls and our guilt. But Jesus, it seems, wasn't talking about people's souls, he was talking about their money. The nearest translation of what he actually said seems to be 'forgive us our debts'. Let our debts be cancelled. This may mean little to those who can pay off their credit card accounts each month, but it meant everything to the mass of the people Jesus encountered.

Jesus was saying: pray the crushing burden of debt that is driving you to an early grave might be cancelled. But more than that: by implication, he is saying God cares about worldly issues like bread and debt. God cares about whether you have a roof over your head, and whether you are treated with respect and accorded basic human dignity. No wonder the crowds flocked to hear him. Little wonder the powerful were becoming concerned about this peasant from 'up north' in Galilee.

The things he said

It's easy for a journalist to pick out juicy quotes to dramatise a story, so maybe we need ask whether the examples we've been exploring are the exception or the rule. What else did Jesus say and do that might add to our increasingly unchurchy picture of him?

One of his favourite ways of talking to the crowds who gathered to hear him were short stories called parables. The Church has traditionally interpreted the parables as illustrations of the nature of God and what his rule or 'kingdom' might be. Thus the parable of the labourers in the vineyard has been seen as portraying God as generous and kind. Treating each person equally, regardless of their abilities.

The story in Matthew's Gospel (chapter 20, verses 1-16) is about the owner of a vineyard who needs help gathering the harvest of grapes. Early in the morning he goes to the market place and hires two men, agreeing to pay them the day labourers' rate of one denarius. But by midday it is clear the work will not be completed in time, so the landowner goes back and hires two more men. At teatime the work is still not finished, so again the landowner goes and hires another two men. At the end of the day, when the grapes are all gathered in, he pays each of the men, starting with the pair who were hired last.

Even though they have only worked for a couple of hours, to their surprise, they receive the full day's pay: one denarius. They take the money and run before the landowner changes his mind – or realises his mistake. Then the landowner comes to the men who have worked since midday and, surprisingly, pays them the same: one denarius. They too leave, but not very happily since they expected to receive more. Finally the landowner comes to the men who have worked all day in the hot sun –

and gives them one denarius each. At this point, the two labourers complain angrily that they should have received more than the others. But the landowner says: Friend, I have done you no wrong. You agreed to work for one denarius. Take what belongs to you and go.

Down the years the Church has interpreted this parable roughly as follows. The landowner is God and the vineyard is his created world. He calls us to work in his world and we receive life. For those who come to faith late in their lives, the reward is still the same because God is equally generous to all.

It seems Matthew shared this interpretation because he prefaces the story by saying 'The Kingdom of heaven is like. . .'. But Matthew and the later Church have forgotten about the Onion. Lay this parable alongside the onion diagram and something very surprising happens.

The landowner with the vineyard is wealthy. We know this because grapevines take several years to grow before they produce a harvest – and give a return on investment. Grapes are a luxury item that are made into wine, a commodity easily exported and converted into money. The vineyard is not an example of subsistence farming, it is a profit-generating enterprise requiring a long-term outlay of capital.

But where does the wealth of the rich come from? The exploitation of the poor. The landowner offers the workers the daily rate of one denarius. That was just enough to live on for a day. But the impoverished labourers were not guaranteed work every day – or for the whole of a day. Much of the work was seasonal – grapes only ripen once a year. So they were being offered below subsistence wages, even at harvest time when the demand for labour would have been at its peak.

In order to keep their wages low, it is in the interests of employers to discourage casual workers from combining to form anything resembling a trade union. United they could be in a position to bargain for better pay rates. Divide and rule has always been a profitable business strategy. So what does the landowner do? He divides and rules. It costs him fractionally more than would otherwise have been the case, but it is well worth the expense.

Note how the labourers are paid. The last come first when it is time to be paid and they make off with their unexpected winnings. But the men who have worked longer hours are angry with the landowner and envious of the labourers who worked fewer hours. Worker solidarity is destroyed.

However, there is worse to come. The landowner challenges the men who dared to protest. He says: 'Am I not allowed to do what I choose with what belongs to me?' (verse 15). But does the land (and the resulting wealth) really belong to him? Almost certainly it has been taken from the poor as the rich accumulated large land holdings and small farmers were often driven into poverty and subsistence level wages. In a way he was paying the labourers from what was rightfully theirs.

Then the landowner delivers a killer blow. He says to the most rebellious labourer: Friend, take what belongs to you and go. But the word that translates as 'friend' is not a gentle word. It is an expression of hostility, in the same way that two men having a bitter argument in a bar might refer to each other as 'pal' – the word is sarcastic and spat out.

The landowner dismisses the rebellious labourers, saying take the money and go. Go, as in don't come back here asking for work. Go, as in you will never get work in this area again when other employers hear about your impudence. Go, as in banishment. Go to your ruin.

So why did Jesus tell this story? What was he doing? It is possible that he was confronting the poor with the injustice that ensured they remained in poverty. Like Steve Biko, making them conscious of their predicament and encouraging them to think of a way to challenge that injustice.

People living in poverty can often be in denial about their situation. Homeless people I have known, sleeping rough on the streets, would sometimes deny they were either poor or homeless. It was a way of clinging on to their human dignity. A way of reducing the pain that was a constant part of their daily lives.

I may sound disturbing, but Jesus wasn't so much interested in pain reduction as challenging and removing structural injustice.

Life and death

Three other stories hammer home what Jesus was doing when he told these subversive parables and, in a strange way, they fit together in a progression of rising optimism and hope.

The first is a story about Lazarus, a poor man so close to death that he can never find justice on earth. In Luke chapter 16, verses 19-31, Lazarus sits, week in week out, begging at the gate of a rich man. But the rich man is so heartless that he will not even give him the scraps of food that fall from his table. Then, one day, the rich man and Lazarus both die. Lazarus, the beggar, is carried up to heaven, but the rich man is consigned to a place of suffering where, unwisely, he is still issuing orders and making demands.

Jesus tells this story as a stark warning to the rich. It would certainly be a memorable image next time the crowds encountered the wealthy and powerful or felt ground down by poverty.

The second story is called the parable of the talents (Matthew chapter 25, verses 14-30). A rich man gives each of three servants money to invest while he goes away on a journey. The first two invest his money cleverly and reap a large reward for him, but the third servant buries the money he has been given in the ground. When the rich man returns he praises the first two for their enterprise, but the third is condemned for his idleness.

The Church's traditional interpretation of this story is that the rich man is God, who gives each of us gifts to use in his service. Those who use their gifts well will be praised, but those who are idle and waste their 'talents' will be held to account and punished.

However, our onion diagram gives rise to a completely different interpretation. To those who live comfortable lives this alternative version appears strange but to people experiencing poverty in first-century Palestine it might have been obvious. This is the Onion version:

As with the story of the labourers in the vineyard, the rich man has obtained his wealth by exploiting the poor. His interest, as ever with the rich, is to increase his wealth still further. He gives money to his servants and orders them to make more money for him in his absence. It is an exercise in venture capitalism. But from whom will this new money be made? The poor.

The first two servants cooperate fully in the extension of the rich man's profit-making enterprise and are well rewarded for their success. In this way thriving business empires are created. The third servant, however, goes away and buries the money he has been given in the ground. Is he simply lazy or is he defying the rich man and refusing to engage in the exploitative task he has been given? Is he a rebel challenging a capitalist system that is key to the social order?

When it comes to the reckoning, the third servant bravely, or perhaps foolishly, accuses the rich man of ruthlessly exploiting those who are economically vulnerable. His wealthy employer is furious at this act of defiance and the servant is cast into the outer darkness, which might mean permanent unemployment, starvation and ultimate death.

Jesus may be saying that, despite the personal cost, some people are still courageous enough to challenge the system. Be inspired by their example. He might even have been talking about himself.

A feisty woman

Our third story is about a very determined woman who demanded, and eventually received, justice from an unjust judge. Luke tells the story (chapter 18, verses 1-8) just a few pages after the Lazarus account. The gospel writer assumes the parable is about the need to persist in prayer even when our prayers do not seem to be answered. But it may be about something much more down to earth.

The story is that the woman, a person of low social status in the ancient world, goes to the powerful judge to demand justice against an adversary. Judges were frequently in the pay of the wealthy and powerful, so it was often extremely difficult for the poor to obtain justice. Predictably, the arrogant (male) judge refuses to hear the woman's case and sends her away with a flea in her ear.

Most people might have given up at that rebuttal, but the woman battles on. Undeterred, she keeps coming back, relentlessly renewing her demand for justice. At last, in exasperation, the judge gives in. 'I will vindicate her, or she will wear me out by her continual coming', he says (verse 5).

Maybe the story reveals how Jesus thought the poor should challenge social and economic injustice. Not by armed struggle but by a relentless demand for what is right. A refusal to admit defeat in the face of overwhelming opposition. A refusal to be beaten down and humiliated.

Years ago when I worked for an ecumenical social justice project I began to think our struggle for justice was hopeless. Faced by a powerful government intent on damaging the lives of vulnerable people and a wealthy institutional Church that seemed happy to walk past on the other side, it was tempting to pack it all in.

The odds were stacked massively against us but I remember someone saying: We must never give in. We must be relentless in demanding justice. No matter what happens we will never accept defeat.

From the outset, Jesus is on a collision course with the rich and powerful. Not only is he saying these issues of justice and freedom are his agenda, but that they are God's agenda. So, if Jesus is who some people think he is, that seems to suggest God may also be on a collision course with the powerful.

With that sort of vision set before us, the struggle for justice might not be hopeless after all.

3

Food for thought

Jesus brought new hope to the poor and marginalised not only by what he said but also by his actions. Reading the gospel accounts, one of the things we see him doing repeatedly is sharing food with people. All sorts of people. We know that sharing a meal with others is a sign of friendship and trust, especially in the Middle East. But the meals Jesus shared were frequently with outcasts: the people whom society decreed were beyond acceptance, trust and friendship.

Time and again in the Gospels we see him being criticised for eating with publicans and sinners. Scandalously, women accused of being involved in prostitution were also welcomed by Jesus. But such conduct was completely inappropriate for a rabbi – a teacher – not least because such outcasts were regarded as being ritually unclean.

For centuries cleanliness had been a major issue in the Jewish faith and a powerful purity code was enforced by the religious authorities. The Temple in Jerusalem was not only intended to be a place of prayer but an instrument for the removal of sins and the restoration of national and personal purity.

On an individual level, wealthy people would have easy access to washing facilities that enabled them to obey the purity law. But the poor, especially the destitute and those working in 'unclean' occupations, were not able to keep to this law. They were stigmatised as unclean and therefore as sinners. People to be avoided as if they had an infection.

But the purity code had also become part of the system of oppression used by the rich as a way of controlling the poor. The argument was that the poor were ritually unclean and therefore did not conform to the law. Therefore they were sinful. If they were sinful, they were worthless and, being worthless, could be exploited freely without provoking inconvenient social criticism.

Rejecting this purity code, Jesus repeatedly shares food with such people – and in the process challenges this key instrument of oppression.

Our onion diagram shows that there was a vast economic and social distance between the richest and poorest. By sharing food with low-status people, Jesus is not simply expressing his love and the love of God for the poor, he is demolishing the barriers that segregate different groups.

But the hierarchical and unjust structure of a society that served the interests of the rich and powerful depended on precisely that segregation. By sharing meals of open fellowship, Jesus is challenging the psychological violence inflicted on the poor that encourages people to believe the poor deserve their poverty. He is challenging oppression and the institutions that maintain it.

Never once does Jesus ask people to repent of their sins before he will share food with them. In fact it is doubtful whether Jesus regarded many of the poor as being sinful at all. And the same is true today.

Among my friends is a very courageous young woman who, in the past, was forced into prostitution. She was looked down on by many respectable people but I am privileged to know her background story. She had been physically and sexually abused as a young child. As a result she was placed in local authority care for her own protection. But staffing at the children's home was inadequate to say the least. Pimps frequently cruised around that area of the city and before long she was picked up.

The pimps gave her things she had seldom experienced: attention and affection. They bought her nice clothes and took her to parties. They told her they loved her and that she was special. They gave her sweets and cigarettes and had sex with her. They persuaded her to experiment with drugs and soon she was hooked on heroin. Then she was made to go out and work as a prostitute on the streets of the city. She was very young: still a child. Just the way the punters like them. If she protested, she was punished severely. When she tried to run away, they beat her savagely.

In the eyes of the law, and of the general public, she was a prostitute. She had no one to turn to and nowhere to hide. Years later she managed to escape and began, with great courage, to rebuild her life.

Looking back on her story I find it hard to identify any action she willingly engaged in that was sinful. The sin was on the part of those who controlled her, but the stigma still lingers. For years such abused and exploited women have been regarded as 'common prostitutes' and shunned by the rest of society for their immoral life. But many of them, like my friend, are survivors not offenders. The real offenders are the enterprising pimps who drive around in their flashy cars, always on the prowl for vulnerable children they can lure into abusive situations.

I wonder whether the burning anger I feel at that situation was also felt by Jesus. And with what satisfaction he shared food with similar survivors of sexual and economic exploitation. It is an honour to be accepted as a friend by that young woman, and I sometimes wonder whether Jesus also felt honoured that such people would eat with him – and befriend him. His actions infuriated the rich as they saw another bulwark of their power being symbolically and systematically undermined. This wasn't tea and sympathy: it was revolution – and the rich knew it.

The problem with miracles

One key aspect of the gospel most people find difficult to accept follows on from the subversive fellowship meals of Jesus: namely his miracles. Is there such a thing as a miracle? What actually happened when Jesus apparently healed people? And how do the healing miracles fit with the Onion?

For the Church the healing miracles are physical expressions of the love of God engaging in the here and now. They are also important demonstrations of the authority of Jesus. So far so good. But did they happen as medical events?

Think about what was going on in first-century Palestine – and what is still going on in the world today. Think back to questions we have already touched on. What happens to a population when it suffers military occupation? When poverty is imposed by the rapacious greed of the rich and the endless demands for produce from the oppressed? What happens when there is a sense of abandonment by God and a gross betrayal by the religious leaders who collude with the rich?

What happens when the earthly focus of worship, the Temple in Jerusalem, is transformed into a warehouse for goods stolen from God's people? What happens when people who dare to rebel are executed by the powerful elite? What happens when a child hears of, or even witnesses, naked bodies decomposing on crosses at the roadside, and fears that such a death might come to its own family?

Fear heightens awareness. But where does the fear and the trauma go when there seems no end to the nightmare? When you are locked in to a living hell? At least in situations of all-out war, there can often be a sense of national solidarity. That, for better or for worse, we are all in it together. But with military occupation, when oppression masquerades as peace, people often feel isolated. That's when the real nightmares begin.

We get a hint of this in Matthew's Gospel (chapter 9, verse 36) where it says that Jesus had compassion on the crowd because they were 'harassed and helpless, like sheep without a shepherd'.

But what happens when this sense of helplessness and oppression reaches a critical level? In Mark's Gospel (chapter 5, verses 1-20) we see what may be the catastrophic result of extreme distress and anxiety. Jesus is confronted by a man who lives wild among the tombs. He is so violent that no one is able to control him and no one dares come near for fear of him. He has ripped his clothes to shreds as his anger turns in on himself and even gashed his own flesh with sharp stones in outbursts of furious self-harm.

But somehow in his encounter with Jesus, the man is healed. Maybe there is a clue in Mark's account as to what may have caused his mental anguish. In the process of healing Jesus asks him his name. My name is Legion, the man replies. Who cares what his name is? Did it matter? Perhaps it did. The root of the word means 'many' but to most people living in first-century Palestine 'legion' would inevitably conjure up an image of the Roman legions: the instrument of brutal political and psychological oppression. Could it be that the man was 'possessed' by a mental illness caused by multiple trauma associated with the Roman military?

The story ends with Jesus sending the 'unclean spirits' into a herd of pigs which rushed into the sea and were drowned. Whether that really happened or whether it was an editorial elaboration by the gospel writer, we do not know. But, without doubt, that is exactly what an oppressed and traumatised people would want to happen to an alien army: that it would disappear across (or under) the sea and never come back.

A new vision

Jesus is frequently pictured driving out evil spirits from people possessed by demons. Today few people in the western world believe in evil spirits or demons, but we do recognise psychological trauma. And we are increasingly aware of the link between psychological trauma and physical symptoms.

Jesus brought the sick and 'the possessed' a vision of a different life. He showed them that they were not abandoned by God and that there was a power, an authority and a love greater than that of the Roman Emperor and the relentless greed of the rich. That they were not alone. In that encounter people were healed in mind and perhaps also in body. They were no longer be paralysed by fear and hopelessness.

In first-century Palestine, physical and mental paralysis was almost certainly made worse by a sense of sin. The idea that illness and affliction were a punishment for disobeying God. Remember the story of the man who was lowered through the roof of a house on his stretcher because the people crowding round Jesus were blocking the way? Standing in the dust and rubble of the badly damaged roof, Jesus tells the man his sins are forgiven. But was the paralysed man a notorious sinner? Or was his paralysis caused, at least in part, by a belief that he was being punished by a vengeful God?

Maybe Jesus was telling the man that, whatever sins people had convinced him had caused his paralysis, they were taken away. He was liberated from that belief and mindset. Often Jesus tells people their own faith has healed them: empowering people and handing back to them self-respect and self-determination. But if Jesus did heal people, why didn't he heal *all* of the people? Why didn't he wave a magic wand and make all of the people well again? Perhaps the answer was that, firstly, he wasn't a magician. Secondly he wasn't primarily interested in making sick people well.

The clue might be in the healing of Peter's mother-in-law (Mark 1:30, 31). When people heard what had happened, they brought their own sick friends and neighbours to Jesus. He heals them but very early the next morning he leaves town. He has his own agenda and it is about much more than healing. On the occasions when he does heal people, he typically sends them back to their own communities. Where they go, we are not told. They disappear from our sight. And that might be the key.

On the move

There's a thread running through the Gospels that is easily missed. Jesus never seems to stay in the same place for very long. He's always on the move. Nowhere is special to him, apart from Jerusalem. And that place is only special because it is the centre of corruption and oppression. What Jesus seems to be demonstrating by his constant travelling is that no place and no building is more important than another. No more special to God.

'The Kingdom of Heaven is among *you*,' he tells the people. Emerging, being affirmed and lived out here and now in the dust of this peasant village. He takes a child and puts it in the centre of the crowd and says: this kid that society regards as worthless, is a symbol of the kingdom. And he probably meant that in more ways than one.

Think about it. What do children do? They run around. They play. They squeal and shout, bursting with energy. For a moment one of them is still and quiet as Jesus speaks about her or him. But what happens moments later? The child is released and races off to join the others. Perhaps it is that explosion of energy and laughter, and not the heavy solemnity of the institutional Church, that captures the essence of God's kingdom.

In the kitchen

There is a refreshing and important equality or egalitarianism about Jesus when it comes to people and places that is the polar opposite of hierarchy. An idea that would not be welcomed by the rich and powerful for whom hierarchy was the vehicle for their high visibility wealth and status.

But Jesus tended to prefer low visibility; sometimes even invisibility. He once said that God's kingdom was like the yeast that someone making bread kneads into the dough. The yeast disappears from sight but it is the silent working of the yeast that makes the bread rise and become edible.

Jesus worked exactly like that yeast: allowing his vision of hope and justice to spread quietly among the people: not by fanfare and proclamation but whispered by word of mouth, from house to house, village to village. As yeast raises the heavy dough, so the vision of Jesus raises the heavy hearts of the poor.

From the moment he read the passage from the book of the prophet Isaiah in the synagogue, Jesus was a marked man as far as the authorities were concerned. The problem was that he was a moving target, constantly on the move from one village to another. It was impossible to predict when he might turn up next.

He told stories and said that, hearing them, 'they' might not understand. But who were the *they* he speaks of? Maybe the informers working for the authorities who heard what he said but couldn't figure out what he was getting at. For the common people, however, the meaning would be clear – and sometimes deliciously amusing.

There is no better example of this than the story of Jesus being challenged by the powerful as to whether it was right to pay taxes to Caesar. Jesus replies: Give to Caesar what is due to him and to God what is due to God (Matthew 22:21).

The Church usually takes this to be an argument for obedience to the civil authorities, but the crowd listening to Jesus might have disagreed. They knew full well that absolutely everything is owed to God, the giver of life. On the other hand, as far as they were concerned, the only thing due to Caesar, the robber of the world and oppressor of the poor, was a prison cell.

Jesus lived in a world similar in some respects to ours, where many men instinctively seek greatness. To be a winner, to be the best, to get to the top. Jesus however referred to himself, not as the Son of God (a title used by Caesar in an attempt to assert his own divinity) but as the 'son of man' and the servant of others.

Jesus seems to have chosen to operate from the grassroots, gradually sowing the seeds of a new hope and a new vision. The fact that this vision was highly subversive as far as the power elite were concerned made it imperative that he remained free to move around for as long as possible.

It is not hard to imagine the effect of this tactical mobility on the local population when Jesus suddenly arrives and then, just as quickly, disappears down the road. How the gossip would have spread. The stories of healing. The parables that made people think and question. The words that gave hope. The simple deeds that threatened the structures of religious and military power. Deeds all but lost in the gospel narratives.

One day he heals a leper (Mark chapter 1, verses 40-42). But in the instant *before* the healing takes place, Jesus reaches out and touches the man. In that moment, the purity law is broken and this rabbi, who the common people are beginning to think is much more than that, is himself defiled. One moment of courageous loving solidarity and acceptance would be the talk of the village, and the surrounding villages, for a lifetime.

Jesus is restoring the minds of the people so that they are free at last from the psychological tyranny that oppressed them. The effect of this unexpected release must have been one of incredulity and of joy. Sometimes laughter can be a subversive antidote to fear and oppression, and Jesus would have been well aware of that.

4

Jesus and gender justice

It is said that to understand another person we need to walk in their shoes: to experience the world from their viewpoint. This is particularly true of understanding the situation of people living in poverty.

That's why we ran retreats on the streets and other experience-based courses on urban spirituality in Leeds. It gave middle class churchgoers from the leafy suburbs an insight into how some of their fellow citizens lived, what God might be thinking of it all and what the implications of 'love your neighbour' might be.

It was only years later I discovered that what is true of another person's shoes is also true when it comes to sanitary towels. I had to start wearing them.

Being told you have cancer is an interesting experience. It's like suddenly being transported into another world. I was one of the lucky ones: mine was prostate cancer. The operation was straightforward and, hopefully, successful. One of the side-effects, however, is that for several months you become incontinent. So you are issued with absorbent pads. Pads that need changing regularly. In a toilet: one with cubicles.

Normally men have it easy. You walk into a loo, unzip, have a wee and walk out. Even if you stay to wash your hands, it only takes a couple of minutes. But pads take much longer. And used pads need to be disposed of appropriately. Suddenly everything gets more complicated. And, if the pad gets too full, potentially humiliating. I was learning fast.

Then, one day I made a big mistake. I said to my wife: 'I realise now what women have to put up with.' She gave me one of her serious looks. 'How's the pain?' she asked. 'Pain? I haven't got any pain,' I said. Then I shut up. I thought about what it might be like if, instead of an inconvenient bladder, I had an excruciatingly painful menstrual period. And what it might be like for that to happen for a whole week, every month. For thirty or forty years. With pads that filled with not a sterile, colourless liquid but with blood. Blood that can stain clothing. Blood that drains energy from the body.

Then there's the money. I got my pads on the NHS, free of charge. But how I would have managed if I had to buy my pads? If I was a woman on benefits, or living in poverty in the Third World and couldn't afford pads at all? What would I use? Toilet paper? Rags? Bits of old newspaper? Grass? How would I feel if powerful, influential people looked down on me and said my monthly menstrual cycle was unclean, and therefore sinful?

That got me thinking about other, even more serious gender issues. For example, development agencies report that, across the world, more women of childbearing age die from acts of male-inflicted violence than are killed by malaria, cancer and road accidents put together? It seems there's an invisible gender war going on. But how did it come to this, or was it always so?

The blame game

For a moment we need to step a long way back in time. In the far distant past many, if not most, human groups were nomadic: always on the move. Survival depended on constantly seeking out water and new grazing for their sheep and cattle. It is highly likely that the ability to discern 'the way' that led to new pastures was shared by both men and women. Because women tended to live longer, it may be they acquired the greater wisdom and knowledge. Such women would have had significant status in the group, often perhaps as leaders.

Then, about ten thousand years ago, came the dawn of agriculture. Communities that had once been nomadic gradually settled in fixed locations where the ground was particularly fertile. Primitive agriculture may well have been started by women as they foraged for food close to their settlements.

However, over time, as agricultural methods improved, surplus produce began to accumulate. With that accumulated wealth came power. And hierarchy. Land became a measure of wealth and of status. Territory was vital in an agrarian economy and had to be defended. Men were physically stronger than women and a warrior class developed. Military leadership led to kingship and greatly increased inequalities in both wealth and gender status.

Meanwhile, interlocking with these economic and political changes, communal narratives were being created and shared. Stories that reflected on the community's origins. Heroism and success were celebrated, while disaster and misfortune needed to be rationalised and explained. People needed an answer to the eternal question: why are things as they are? And, in particular, why do bad things happen?

One gender-loaded answer came around 700BCE when the Greek poet Hesiod wrote a story about a beautiful woman called Pandora. Pandora, the first woman created by the gods, was given a jar that contained all the evils in the world. The gods warned her that she must never open the jar. But, tempted by curiosity, Pandora did just that. Immediately the evils flew out and spread throughout the world. It was impossible to get them back in the jar.

It is not difficult to see the gender allusion inherent in this fictional story: the woman beautiful but apparently weak; the jar representing the woman's sexuality which, once opened, allowed all evil to emerge. The consequent blame for all the world's ills heaped on her.

A century or so later in another part of the Middle East, the Old Testament book of Genesis was being composed. It contains a remarkably similar story. Eve, the first woman, is created by God. She is warned not to eat of the fruit of the tree of life. But Eve is tempted by a snake and eats the forbidden fruit. Then she tempts Adam to do the same. Disaster ensues: sin enters the world because of her.

When was the book of Genesis written? At the time the Hebrews had been conquered and taken into captivity by the Babylonians. It was a time of national disaster. A time when some sort of explanation, real or imaginary, was needed. From that point on, the concept of sin and punishment seems to become significantly more prominent in the consciousness of the Hebrews.

Whether the stories of Pandora and Eve have any historical basis is not the issue here. What matters is that we humans have a need to know why things happen. In particular misfortune needs to be explained. And, psychologically, it helps if blame can be attached to someone. In both cases that someone is Woman. The stories may not be factually true but the gender stereotyping is very real and continues to this day.

Those most sinned against in a powerful patriarchal world end up being portrayed as the source of sin. Very often, the victim is blamed for the injustice and the perpetrator is exonerated.

Girls and boys

So what was happening at the time of Christ when it came to gender? The answer starts with conception. There was the belief in the ancient world (continuing well into the Victorian era) that conception was like planting a seed in the ground. The male sperm was the seed and the woman's womb was the earth, the germinating environment.

She was the receptacle for the new life which, it was believed, was wholly contained in the male seed. It was the man who gave life. He was the active, potent, god-like creator: the woman was the secondary, passive incubator. Then came the birth. There would be rejoicing if the child was a boy, but often disappointment if it was a girl.

In the Roman world a female newborn baby was regarded as being so worthless that it might be simply be thrown on a rubbish heap to die from exposure or to be eaten by wild animals. In first-century Palestine, girls were also of low status. A father was entitled to sell a daughter as a slave for a period of seven years. Those who remained in the house were expected to act as servants. Often they were required to wash their father's face and feet – the typical duty of a female slave.

Women and girls were under the control of male members of the household and were forbidden to go out alone or unveiled in case dishonour was brought on the family. Women who did go out alone or who spoke to men outside the family group were in danger of being accused of sinfulness. A girl was not allowed to refuse a man in marriage and a woman could be divorced by her husband at will if she displeased him or if she did not bear children. Failure to produce children was deemed to be the fault of the woman. It was assumed that her apparent barrenness was a punishment for sin. A woman was not permitted to divorce her husband.

As we can see from the words of the Ten Commandments, women were regarded as little more than chattels – the property of men:

'Neither shall you covet your neighbour's wife, his slave, his slave girl, his ox, his donkey, or anything that *belongs* to him.' (Deuteronomy 5:21, NEB)

Further problems emerged as children got older. With good fortune, the average smallholding might be big enough to support a growing family but, when it came to inheritance, the farm would be too small to divide up in viable economic units among the children. In such a case the eldest son would inherit the smallholding and the other children would have to leave. Younger sons would typically become day labourers on large estates or hope to learn a trade. Girls might become domestic servants in larger households or, failing that, forced to live by begging or prostitution.

As the wealthy and powerful increasingly bought out smaller farms, this process was becoming acute in the time of Jesus. So what was his reaction to all this? The gospel accounts were almost certainly all written by men. But, even so, if we look carefully, we can see Jesus making some powerful and very controversial comments about gender equality. And sometimes his most powerful and eloquent comments were non-verbal.

As we have seen, reading the Gospels, one is struck by the number of times Jesus is accused of eating with sinners. We might pause to wonder how many of those sinners were women. We know that a number of women followed Jesus, some of whom may have been forced into prostitution or were referred to as sinners simply because they had the courage to go out in public on their own – and the nerve to associate with a religious outcast like Jesus!

One key passage of scripture that refers to divorce is Mark 10, verses 1-9. Here Jesus is pictured saying that in marriage two people become one flesh and that divorce is against the will of God. Even the law of God? But Jesus is a notorious law-breaker. He is often being attacked by the religious leaders for breaking the purity code and for healing on the Sabbath. Was he really saying that there are no circumstances in which a couple in a destructive marriage may not divorce?

We don't know the answer to that question, but what we do know is that divorce wasn't the issue that would have upset people most. The men anyway. What does Jesus say? That the man and woman become one flesh. One indivisible person. But men regarded women as items of property, to be retained if it pleased them or discarded by a simple bill of divorce if it did not. That gross inequality was a major cause of fear and suffering among women. In a moment you could become homeless and destitute – and branded as a sinner into the bargain.

This brief passage has massive implications for us. If Jesus is saying that, in marriage, the two people become, as it were, part of each other then there must be a radical equality of rights, value and status between the man and woman.

So what more controversy is Jesus stirring up?

Provocative prayer

One of the most dangerous words in the world is normality: the idea that things that are familiar are also safe and acceptable.

There are few things more normal to a Christian than the Lord's Prayer. We say it so often that many of us seldom give it a thought. But the people who first heard it probably gave it a lot of thought. We think of the prayer as the Our Father, but it seems that is not what Jesus intended. The word he used was Abba – the equivalent of Daddy. However, to use that word when addressing God would have been shocking, and for some people dangerously provocative.

For a start, it blew apart the idea of hierarchy on which the whole of society was based. If you could address God in such a trusting and intimate way, then the hierarchical status of the rich and powerful paled into insignificance. Abba was a word whose intimacy might have been normal in addressing a mother. But that wasn't the image of God Jesus was suggesting: or was it?

Things are equally enigmatic when you get further on in the prayer where we come to the words: Give us today our daily bread. What are the two absolute essentials for life? Bread and, especially in a hot climate, water. Jesus is telling the crowds, most of whom would be poor, to pray for life: for survival. Pray that you may receive. But from whom?

Who cooked the food in a first-century Palestinian household? Who put the bread on the table? The women. And the water that people needed to drink? Who was it that was made to carry the water? Even though water is extremely heavy, it was the women. Think of the story of Jesus and the woman at the well. A woman, not a man.

Preparing food and providing water was women's work. Humble work that a servant or slave might do for us if we were rich and powerful. But Jesus seems to be saying this is work in which God participates.

How does the idea of God as servant fit with the model of hierarchy on which the Roman Empire depended? It doesn't.

Then there is the story of the returning prodigal son (Luke 15:11-32). The father sees the disgraced son while he is still far off and runs to meet him. He flings his arms round him, despite the filth of pigs on the boy's clothes. 'We must celebrate,' he tells the servants. 'This son of mine was dead but is alive.'

We naturally assume the father has forgiven the son. But he hasn't. It's strange but in the story the father doesn't even speak to the son. There is no word of forgiveness for wasting the family's money or for bringing disgrace on the family. For endangering the economic viability of the farm.

No word of forgiveness? How can that be? Is the father still angry? Quite the opposite. Forgiveness involves counting the cost. If you take a paper clip off my desk it does not matter. You may technically have stolen it but I don't mind. The cost is so insignificant that I don't care. It would sound utterly ridiculous if I were to say to you: 'I forgive your dishonesty in stealing that paper clip.'

But the son had wasted a huge slab of the family's money. Money his parents had worked all their lives to save. All that effort had been thrown away. Why didn't that money and that disgrace matter to the father? Because at that moment, with his arms round his son, holding on for dear life and desperately trying not to burst into tears of joy in front of the servants, those things paled into insignificance *compared with* the boy's life. So great is the father's love that, compared to the son's survival, money and honour are no more than a paper clip.

Imagine the crowd walking home after hearing that parable and discussing what it meant. When one of the men arrives back he tells his wife about the story Jesus has told. The father running to meet the son and, instead of being angry with him, hugging the boy.

'I'd never have done that,' says the husband.

'No dear, but I would,' replies his wife.

Behaving like a typical man, the father might well have punished the son or at least made him realise exactly how much his foolishness had cost the family in money and honour. He might then have grudgingly forgiven him. But the sense of indebtedness would have lingered. The son might have felt deep gratitude but it would have been an obligatory gratitude that could never be forgotten.

But as Jesus tells it, the situation is so completely flooded out with love that there is no room for blame or balance sheets.

If the father in the parable represents God, then what might that mean? Alarmingly, it may mean that God does not want our eternal grovelling gratitude. God simply wants us to know that we are loved: overwhelmingly and without condition. But that isn't typically manly. Not much there about masculine strength and assertiveness. In fact it sounds rather womanly.

Nuts and bolts

When we spoke of the ancient belief that the man's seed contained the whole of human life we passed discreetly over the actual act of procreation. But now we need to think for a moment about the nuts and bolts of that process. The act of procreation involves penetration. That word is very important to most men. They get gratification from it. A sense of potency and self-worth.

Unfortunately, that psychological need for success extends far beyond the marital bed. Military success depends on penetration: of the enemy's territory and towns, but also of the enemy's body. Think how many weapons of war are in the shape of a penis or have a penetrative function: a spear, a rifle, a bullet, a torpedo, a guided missile, a bomb. Instruments of domination, conquest, violence, cruelty and acquisitiveness.

If a man penetrates a woman, he gives life. If he penetrates his enemy he brings victory and achieves dominance. Powerful stuff. Just the way many people pictured God. As a mighty warrior.

Research indicates that many men are attracted to violence because it gives them a sense of power and control. But maybe also because they are basically weak? Fearful of their own inadequacy: hence the need to dominate? As the Roman philosopher Seneca said: 'All cruelty springs from weakness.'

In the parable of the prodigal son, Jesus does not describe the father as assertive and thrusting. He does not demand apology, revenge or restitution. He does not behave like a conventional father but like a typical mother. Only someone with the greatest respect for women would dare to do that.

First and last

As we explore the Gospels we keep stumbling over these situations where Jesus appears to be saying something quite 'normal' but then almost tricking us or teasing us into making a new discovery when it comes to gender.

In Luke's Gospel, the public ministry of Jesus begins with him declaring that he has been sent by God to proclaim good news to the poor, release for the captives and sight for those who cannot see. That sounds fairly straightforward. But then an interesting question arises. Was Jesus aware that more than half the people living in poverty were women? Did his words not just include women, but did they apply *especially* to women? Did they have a particular power and resonance for women?

What was good news for them? Freedom from the tyranny of patriarchy. From the captivity of servitude under male domination. A new vision of hope for women who could see no way out of their domestic and public suffering.

One of Jesus' most memorable sayings was that the last shall be first (Luke chapter 13, verse 30). This comment was likely to have alarmed the rich and powerful but to have given a spark of hope to the poorest.

But who among the poor *were* the poorest? Who are the poorest in any community in the world today? The poorest in terms of power, status and wealth are almost always the women.

(This profound and enduring injustice is likely to prove catastrophically significant as the effects of climate change kick in. Global warming will affect the poor far more than the rich. The wealthy will be able to afford basic precautions such as moving to geographically safer areas, but among the poor, the poorest will suffer most. As ever this will disproportionately affect women and children. However, as we shall see, it may be exactly from among those people that the answer to this growing crisis may ultimately emerge.)

Was Jesus aware of this same gender disparity when it came to power, self-determination and, ultimately, survival? Of course he was. So what was he up to? He was challenging a powerful stereotype, working to undermine another system of injustice. Giving a vision of a different order in which women would no longer be ill-treated as the property of men.

Women should be raised up not just because they suffer the greatest poverty but because they reflect the nature of God. However, that is not an idea that would have endeared itself to men in first-century Palestine – or the early Church.

Of course, the counter argument to this suggestion is that Jesus is the perfect image and reflection of God and Jesus was a man. Well – perhaps. Think of the times Jesus is portrayed by the gospel writers as being in a servant role. At the Last Supper the imagery is that of Jesus blessing and distributing the bread. Forget for a moment what he might or might not have said when he did that: what might his action have conveyed? It was the man's role to say the blessing over the bread, but it was a woman's job to hand out the food at a meal. Was Jesus being womanly in *giving* the bread to the disciples?

Then we come to the fourth Gospel. Amazingly St John omits the account of the Last Supper as we have it in the earlier Gospels. Instead he has the account of Jesus washing the disciples' feet. Washing people's feet? Where have we heard that before?

In a wealthy household there were probably both male and female slaves. But, as we have just seen, in ordinary peasant households, the servant role of foot washing was *female*. The duty of a wife or a daughter. We are familiar with the saying of Jesus that 'I am among you as a servant' but here he is unmistakably pictured choosing the role of a female servant.

What might that have meant? That, in the land of patriarchy, the loud and violent male is dominant, but in the kingdom of God it may be the womanly voice that speaks with real power and authenticity.

How different things might have been if the Church had modelled its ministry on St John's image of the womanly Jesus rather than creating the hierarchical male image of Jesus the priestly mediator.

How different things could be in the future.

5

The Cross

We have seen how Jesus systematically challenged the pillars supporting an unjust and oppressive regime. As his vision of God's 'kingdom' spread, the rich and powerful would have rapidly reached the conclusion that something must be done. One way or another Jesus must be silenced. Hence the crucifixion.

If there is one thing all Christians believe, it is that Jesus died on the cross. The execution of a human being is a very serious matter so any questioning of the death of Jesus and its cause must be treated with the greatest care.

If a journalist was to approach the subject of the cross and resurrection, what might be revealed? They would find that, down the centuries, Christian identity has centred on the death and resurrection of Jesus from the dead, and that most Christians believe they are, in some way, saved by the cross. The Church holds that Jesus died willingly to defeat the evil forces that rule the world and to save humanity from its sins. That this 'salvation' is brought about by, and only by, the death and resurrection of Jesus. That he is, therefore, the 'saviour' of the world. He rescues the world.

In any journalist's language, that is a big story. A sensational story. The Church refers to it as 'the Good News' and down the years it has told that story to the world. But it has omitted to mention the Onion. A journalist writing for a tabloid newspaper might not be interested in the Onion – the background to the story. They might want to focus on the drama, the violence and the blood. Then they would probably do a follow-up piece on the mystery of the strange goings on that occurred 36 hours later.

However, a journalist writing for a 'quality' newspaper would want to ask about the factors that led up to this dramatic series of events. They might even ask about the Onion.

We need to share that journey of exploration. It begins roughly 60 years before the birth of Jesus.

When in Rome

The image most of us have of ancient Rome is of glittering military parades and splendid imperial buildings, but in 60BCE Rome was in a mess. The political structures were breaking down and there was frequent street violence. Rioting often prevented elections being held.

Over the next 30 years there was civil war, murder and intrigue. Finally in 31BCE Augustus became the dictator. For the following 45 years there was political stability. At least on the surface.

One reason for that stability was that Augustus nationalised the army. Instead of owing allegiance to individual generals, the troops were paid by the state. But the size of the massive wages bill (and the pension pot) created a major financial crisis. Especially for the occupied territories.

As a result of the crisis, there was acute pressure on the people at the bottom of the Onion who were taxed to the hilt and robbed of most of the food they managed to grow. But the system worked and there was stability across the empire until the year 14CE when Augustus died.

He was replaced by Tiberius, and it was then that things started to wobble. Tiberius Caesar was a strange man. It seems he didn't like living in Rome and he wasn't very interested in being Emperor. In fact he spent the last decade of his long reign (27 to 37CE) on the island of Capri.

Meanwhile, back in imperial Rome a man called Sejanus was standing in for the emperor. Sejanus liked the power he had been given and wanted more of it. So, in 30CE, he instituted a purge against leading citizens of Rome in a bid for ultimate control. Tiberius swiftly intervened. He ordered Sejanus to be arrested and executed. Then he initiated a furious purge of his own.

In the years that followed, Tiberius was becoming increasingly paranoid and withdrawn. Rome was not only effectively leaderless but it was also troubled by sporadic incursions by Germanic tribes from the north. There must have been a feeling of profound unease among the governing elite.

At the time Jesus set out on his public ministry, in about 30AD, Tiberius was an old man living on far away Capri receiving unsettling reports of turmoil back in Rome. News spread fast across the empire. It was impossible for regional governors, including Pontius

Pilate in Judea, not to have been concerned about those turbulent events. And about their own career prospects.

In the gospel accounts, Pilate is presented as being a weak and indecisive man. According to Matthew's Gospel, he finds no wrong in Jesus and washes his hands of the matter. We find ourselves almost having sympathy for Pilate. But the reality seems to have been quite different. Many historians take the view that Pilate was in fact a harsh and tyrannical agent of Roman oppression, especially against local rebel groups.

In contrast Jesus, a lowly peasant from the northern province of Galilee, always refused to take part in armed uprisings. He presented not the slightest military threat to the Roman rule.

Pilate, aided and abetted by his allies among the Temple hierarchy, was busy making sure that money and produce extracted from the local population flowed smoothly upwards to Rome. Why would he bother with someone like Jesus?

The real threat

The trouble was that Jesus was becoming more dangerous than any armed uprising. He was spreading a new vision of liberation. A vision that challenged hierarchy and gave hope to the oppressed. True, his followers were weak and uneducated, but his vision was spreading among the masses.

He spoke continually of a 'kingdom' of God, in opposition to the kingship of Caesar. This kingdom did not involve military action but arose quietly from among the poor. In the hearts of the oppressed. Its signs were commonplace but powerful. His healing miracles were often accompanied by the insistence that it was the person's faith that had made them well. Words of affirmation and empowerment.

Warnings, delivered by the indigenous religious hierarchy, had done nothing to deter him. In fact, he had used those confrontations to hammer home his message.

People were saying he spoke with authority. The authority of God. But only one person in the Roman Empire claimed such authority and that was Caesar: the man the Roman propaganda machine called 'Son of God and Saviour of the World'.

Pagan tribes on the borders of the empire frequently staged armed uprisings, but, as long as they came with nothing more than swords and spears, Rome was impregnable. If, however, someone opposed the tyranny of Rome with an idea, there could be a problem. Especially if that person refused to back down.

Jesus was the irresistible force and Rome the apparently immovable object. The outcome was inevitable. But what triggered the execution process?

Pilate, powerful as he was, depended on the cooperation of the indigenous tribal leaders for the smooth extraction of money and goods. By this time those local leaders were the sons of Herod the Great, who shared the government of Palestine, and the Temple hierarchy. Not surprisingly, they were extremely angry about the things Jesus was saying and doing: the way he fraternised with sinners, his disregard for the religious purity code, and the way he was destabilising the status quo.

There was also the developing question of who Jesus really was. People were beginning to speak of him as the long-awaited Messiah. The idea of a Messiah, however, raised profound political questions not just of leadership, but of kingship.

These questions must have swirled around the crowds who came to hear him speak, as well as the religious and political hierarchy centred on Jerusalem. Hence the demand to know from Jesus' own lips whether he claimed to be the new king of the Jews. Hence Jesus' assertion that he opposed all such hierarchical thinking.

Rage against the night

A journalist in first-century Palestine, and certainly anyone living 2,000 years later, would be hard put to work out exactly what happened next. What caused the sudden arrest and execution of Jesus?

The Gospels tell us that Jesus, who had spent almost all of his public life in the rural areas among the peasants and the poor, now headed south to the nerve centre of power and oppression: Jerusalem. When he got there he went to the Temple and something happened. The gospel account (Mark 11:15-17) says he turned over the tables of the financial dealers who changed gentile currency into coinage acceptable to the religious authorities, and he condemned the whole Temple as a den of thieves.

It has been pointed out that a single person, or even a small group, could not have brought Temple activity to a halt. In that vast complex of buildings, they would hardly have been noticed. But the action of Jesus had great symbolic power. He physically goes into the central focus of corruption and oppression and denounces it. It is as though he is saying: I have sown the seeds of love and hope in the hearts of the poor. I have given them a vision of God that will inspire and empower them. And now I challenge you and your regime of greed and oppression.

Why was Jesus so foolhardy? To walk into the enemy stronghold and challenge the overwhelming power that was centred there. It seems that Jesus often told his disciples, women and men, not to be afraid. But why might they have been afraid? Because they were in constant danger of arrest and punishment if they followed and shared the revolutionary teaching of Jesus.

There are times in the gospel accounts when Jesus says they must be willing to take up their cross and follow him. That might be a later idea read back into the gospel narrative, or it may have been so clear to Jesus that he felt he must warn his disciples in the starkest of terms what they were getting into. Now, in his last hours, Jesus lives out that reality by confronting, face to face, the powers of oppression.

The poet Dylan Thomas, writing about impending death, urges us to rage against the dying of the light and not to go gently into the darkness. Jesus was not raging against his coming death but he was certainly raging against tyranny and injustice.

Pilate may or may not have been aware of Jesus but, after the incident in the Temple and reports from the religious hierarchy that he was claiming to be a king, the situation would have changed instantly.

Does that mean Pilate was consciously worried that Jesus posed a threat to Roman rule? Not necessarily. All that mattered was that a significant irritation must be removed and the local tribal leaders remain content. And that no reports of a new revolution filter back to Rome. Or to Tiberius on Capri.

The crucifixion

We tend to think that the crucifixion was a one-off event, but people were constantly being crucified in the Roman Empire. Crucifixion was a Roman form of execution designed to inflict massive pain and humiliation, especially on political rebels and runaway slaves.

The gospel accounts of Jesus' crucifixion say that two thieves were executed alongside him. It is more probable, however, that they were political activists or freedom fighters, since few other crimes merited crucifixion. It is said that one of the men shouted abuse at Jesus and the Church has assumed that to be an indication of his corrupt criminal nature. But people in a shared situation of extreme danger and pain often tend to find a bond of solidarity in their distress.

So why was the man angry with Jesus? Perhaps he was one of the zealots who had wanted Jesus to join them in their armed struggle against Rome. It might be the man was angry at what he saw as a lost opportunity. That Jesus, by rejecting the military option, had let the rebels down.

According to the gospel account in Luke, the other so-called thief spoke kindly to Jesus, admitting that he and his compatriot deserved to die. Which, if they were political freedom fighters was, in a sense, true.

But, at this point, a strange question arises. Did Pilate actually want Jesus dead? Pilate, like the Temple hierarchy, certainly wanted the Jesus problem to go away. The Temple hierarchy may have wanted him dead. But did Pilate?

Although Rome had always been a militarised state, the way it dealt with conquered territories was unusual. As we have seen, local leaders were encouraged to collaborate in ruling the newly acquired territory. They were bought off. Enemies were often persuaded to become friends. One of the most famous Jewish rebels, a man called Josephus, changed sides. He became a Roman citizen and a gifted historian.

If Pilate had thought the matter through, he might have wondered whether Jesus as a dead martyr might be even more of a problem to Rome than Jesus alive. But perhaps Jesus could be persuaded to change sides, as had so many others. Looking back, it seems that only one person could ever have stopped the Jesus project and discredited the man, and that was Jesus himself. It was no good other people trying to discredit him. Such attacks simply made him stronger. But if Pilate could follow the tried and tested Roman trick of getting the enemy to change sides, the problem might well be solved.

Maybe the cross was not a punishment but a last-ditch attempt at persuasion. How powerful it would have been if they could have tempted Jesus to change his tune. To confess that it had all been a sham and that he was a fraud. Pilate's hope might have been that Jesus would give in under the extreme pain and ridicule.

But Jesus died. It is said that when the news was taken to Pilate he was surprised that death had come so quickly. But was he surprised, or was he angry that a few more hours of suffering on the cross might have persuaded Jesus to give in? And why was it Jesus had died so quickly? After his arrest, it is likely he sustained significant injuries. The gospel accounts say he was stripped and flogged. He may also have been raped. It is also said that he was beaten about the head. Did he suffer severe head injuries? After all, as with John the Baptist before him, the head was where the dangerous, visionary word of God had come from.

No wonder Jesus needed someone to help carry his cross to the place of execution. One word might have ended all this, but that word of capitulation never came. There was no surrender and no betrayal.

6

Resurrection

The story is well known. Jesus was executed, almost certainly on a Friday afternoon. He died and was buried, possibly around 6pm. The Sabbath began at dusk and his body apparently remained untouched until after the Sabbath had run its course. Then, very early on the morning of the first day of the week, the Sunday, several women went to the tomb. They found it empty. The body had disappeared.

In three of the gospel accounts, Mark, Matthew and Luke, the women say they encountered a young man who told them Jesus had been raised from the dead. In the fourth gospel narrative, Mary Magdalene goes alone to the tomb and finds it empty. She runs and tells Peter and another disciple, described as the one whom Jesus loved. They rush to the tomb. Peter enters first. The second disciple follows and, it is said, he immediately believes Jesus has been raised from the dead. The two disciples leave but Mary remains at the tomb. There, says the gospel writer, she encounters the risen Jesus, mistaking him at first for the gardener.

There follow gospel accounts of several encounters between the disciples and Jesus. Finally, according to Luke, Jesus parts from them. The claim that he was 'taken up' into heaven appears only in a disputed version of the text (chapter 24, verse 51), although St Luke's

Acts of the Apostles begins with the assertion that Jesus was taken up. Why Luke omitted the 'Ascension' from his Gospel is not clear, since he is assumed to also have written Acts.

In what sense any or all of this happened is open to question and the intelligent twenty-first century reader is tempted to reject the idea that such accounts are objectively true statements of actual events.

But our inquiring journalist has to write something and so she or he might start with some basic questions: Did Jesus actually die on the cross? If so, did he physically rise from the dead? If he did, what does that say about Jesus? What effect did this resurrection have on his followers? And, finally, what does it matter to us two thousand years later?

We have no forensic evidence to prove that Jesus did die on the cross, or at any time on Good Friday. However, the Romans were extremely good at killing people and it is likely that he did die. There is also a gospel reference to a soldier plunging a spear into Jesus' side as he hung on the cross. Whether that happened and what damage the spear might or might not have caused to internal organs is not known.

It is said that women (but apparently not the male disciples) were present at the crucifixion and they may have heard the last words of Jesus. If they were present when the body was taken down from the cross after such a relatively short time, it is possible they would have attempted to revive him, had they been given the opportunity. They were hardly likely to treat his physical state with indifference. The fact that, unaccompanied by any male disciples, these women later went to the tomb to clean the body, indicates that there was no expectation of any sort of resurrection.

The most likely explanation for the missing body must be that the Romans or the Temple hierarchy removed it, perhaps to prevent the burial place becoming a shrine and a focus for political unrest. It is possible that the women went to the wrong tomb in the half-light of the early morning, but it is highly unlikely that the right tomb was never found. Either the body was there or it wasn't.

If the Romans or the Temple hierarchy had taken it, they would have said so in order to quash the rumours that Jesus had risen from the dead. If the followers of Jesus took the body, then they would know he had not been raised. Yet the resurrection was central to the rest of their lives, even when that belief was to cause many of them persecution and a violent death. Would they die for a lie, or was some sort of group delusion taking place? Was it all wishful thinking?

That may be a possible explanation. Except that some, if not many of the disciples would know that, somewhere on the outskirts of Jerusalem, the body of a man they loved was rapidly decomposing. Did they simply shut their minds to that grim thought?

What is not in doubt is that belief in the resurrection was accepted by the followers of Jesus (some more readily than others, the gospel accounts admit) and this belief had a massive impact on their lives. For them, it was a powerful affirmation of Jesus as the one sent by God, since only God could have brought about resurrection.

The resurrection became the primary event and the focus for the early Church. The magnitude and brilliance of what they believed had happened was dazzling. If you were to look at the sun for a moment on a cloudless day, you would be dazzled by its brightness. When you looked away you would, for a time, not be able to see anything other than the image of the sun. It would seem as though the image was burned onto your retina.

Maybe something similar to that happened with the Church. For the previous three years, the followers of Jesus had as their focus the things he was doing and saying. Some, particularly the male disciples, seem to have found it difficult always to grasp what he was getting at. Maybe they didn't like to dwell on the warnings of possible suffering his agenda might entail.

There were occasions when Jesus chided them for their stupidity and got exasperated when they seemed to ignore his teaching. Day in and day out he challenged the political and economic hierarchy and its exploitation and degradation of the poor. Reversing the hierarchy of the Roman and the local collaborators, he said the last shall be first and that, to understand and appreciate the kingdom of heaven, you needed to become like a child. But then he found some of the men arguing about which of them would have places of honour in this 'heavenly' kingdom. Clearly they had not been listening. It was not all moonlight and roses.

A perfect sacrifice?

Now everything had changed. The life of Jesus was seen in a completely new light. Instead of proclaiming good news for the poor and release of those held captive by debt, the new proclamation was that Jesus was risen and is Lord of all creation. He is the fulfilment of the Hebrew hope of a Messiah. He is the fulfilment of the Jewish law. Jesus, the dangerous, turbulent messenger of the justice of God for the vulnerable, has become the message itself. It is theologically dazzling: so much so that the future Church seems blinded to what Jesus lived and died for.

Surprisingly, resurrection was not a new concept in the ancient world. In Judaism, the Sadducees rejected the idea but the Pharisees and others believed there would be an eventual resurrection at the end of time. But what nobody seems to have imagined was that it could happen immediately, in the here and now.

After the early Church had accepted the idea that the resurrection of Jesus *had* happened, it started to ask itself what this great act of God meant. Such an amazing event must have a profound meaning. No doubt they thought back to the crucifixion and the sacrifice that Jesus had made in confronting the powers of injustice and oppression, even when he knew it must end in disaster.

Today, we speak of soldiers in conflict situations making the supreme sacrifice, giving their lives in order to save their comrades. But, in Judaism, the concept of sacrifice carried an even more powerful voltage. Sacrifice had been part of Judaism from the earliest times. It may have started in the days when the ancient Hebrews were nomads travelling with their flocks to find green pasture.

In the spring, it seems, they sacrificed a newborn lamb, offering it up to God in thanksgiving for the gift of life. Acknowledging that their survival depended on God's goodness. No doubt these were joyful events.

But in later years, and especially after the exile of the Hebrews in Babylon, sacrifice developed a more sombre character. There was the sense that the captivity of the leading members of Jewish society had been a punishment from God. And to deserve such punishment, they must have sinned greatly.

This deepening awareness of sin related not just to those taken into exile but to the whole of the Hebrew community. Reparation needed to be made to restore their relationship with God. They needed to atone for their failings. It was as though a ransom had to be paid to enable them to be freed from the captivity of sin. Increasingly the Temple ceremonies focused on sacrifice for the restoration of a right relationship with God.

The first followers of Jesus were all Jews, and so this tradition would be deeply embedded in their hearts and minds. It was then a short step to the idea that the crucifixion of Jesus mirrored these sacrifices. The innocent and blameless Jesus was, it seemed, a perfect sacrifice, offered willingly as a substitute for sinful humanity by his own choice. Was that why Jesus went willingly to the cross?

Suddenly there was an escape route away from the dangerous, subversive agenda of Jesus which, as he had warned, was likely to bring suffering and death. Jesus was the ultimate sacrifice that would take away the sins of the Jews. And not only the Jews but, for the writer of the fourth Gospel, the sin of the whole world. Dying on the cross as a perfect sacrificial victim, he became the saviour of his people. The saviour of the world.

Redemption required that the payment offered to restore the object being redeemed must be of equal value. A victim of infinite value to redeem a world of infinite worth. After all, John the Baptist had said: 'Behold the Lamb of God who *takes away the sins* of the world.'

The argument sounds convincing and the imagery attractive. Lambs are normally characterised by passivity and innocence. They are quiet and harmless. They go, we are encouraged to think, without protest to their slaughter. But there are a few details that don't quite fit.

Traditionally, the animal sacrificed in order to take away the sin of the community was a not a lamb: it was a goat (Leviticus chapter 16, verse 20). The 'scapegoat' was symbolically loaded with the sins of the nation, and then sent out into the barren wilderness to die. Taking with it the sins of the people.

Secondly, the famous occasion when lambs were slaughtered was not about sacrifice for sin but about liberation from captivity. The Exodus. According to the Old Testament (Exodus chapter 12, verse 21), the paschal lambs were killed and their blood used to mark the homes of the Hebrew slaves in Egypt.

When the Angel of the Lord came to kill the firstborn of the Egyptians, he saw the blood on the door posts and spared the Hebrew children.

If Jesus is in any sense 'the lamb of God' then his death is about release from slavery and oppression imposed by the rich and powerful, rather than atonement for sin. Which, you might say, fits very well with the Jesus agenda and the Onion. So a Church that extols Jesus as the Lamb of God has, in a way, got it right. It just seems to attach the sacrifice of the cross to the wrong issue.

Could this be so? As we have seen, Jesus was extremely concerned about political and economic oppression, but seems to have been remarkably unconcerned about a lot of human sins. Other than the structural ones committed by the powerful. The story of the speck of sin in the eye of the poor compared to the plank of sin in the eye of the religious leaders, bear witness to that.

The Church might argue that Jesus called people to repent, and today that sounds very much like repenting of our personal sins. But the word 'repent' doesn't only mean being sorry for something, it means (and definitely meant then) turning. Turning away from one course of action or having a different mindset about something. Was that about individual sin? It could have included that, but the force of what Jesus, and John the Baptist before him, were doing was centred on structural injustice.

Jesus was telling the rich and powerful that, in order to have life, they needed to turn away from their oppressive ways. They needed to seek not status but shalom. Peace and well-being in fellowship with their neighbours. And perhaps he was telling the poor that they also must try to have a different mindset. They must try to start believing in themselves and have a vision of a new life. To recognise their own value and worth. It is your own faith that has made you well, he told the woman with the haemorrhage (Mark 5:34).

But the theological experts argue that the death and resurrection of Jesus come as a theological bundle. You cannot understand the one without the other. They say the sacrifice of the cross explains the world-changing miracle of the resurrection, and the resurrection gives ultimate meaning to the cross. Especially when you add in the idea that God gave his own son to be the sacrifice.

The package seems to be powerful and convincing, until our journalist friend asks: 'So, does the loving father of the Lord's Prayer really give his own beloved son as a sacrifice to placate and pay a ransom to . . . himself?' How does that fit with the parable of the prodigal son? Not much by way of ransom and sacrifice there.

Despite that, you can see how it might have come about that the Church has focused on the personal religious issues of sin and redemption rather than on the wider social and political issues of the Onion: the poverty, oppression and debt that the earthly Jesus was concerned with.

Resurrection mattered to the early Church and it is critically important to the Church today. After all, if there was no resurrection, where would the Church be?

Where would we be? And, more to the point, where shall we be when we die?

But now, our journalist might be asking a very disturbing question: does it actually matter whether Jesus was raised from the dead? If the resurrection never happened and the early Church got it wrong, does the whole edifice of Christian theology come crashing down?

One traditionalist argument is that the Church is guided by God, so such an error is not possible. You get the flavour of this from St Paul (of whom more later) when he says that if Jesus is not raised from the dead then '*we* of all people' are most to be pitied. Is the 'we' the early Church or the world?

His sentiment is understandable but it hardly constitutes convincing evidence that the resurrection happened. Here in the twenty-first century, what we want to know is: does it matter whether Jesus was raised from the dead? Because he may well not have been.

The Church would say that, yes it matters to an infinite degree, but the Church has a vested interest in the resurrection being a historical fact. According to most theologians it is central to what the Jesus event is about.

However, other people who believe just as passionately in God and believe Jesus is the human embodiment of God, might say that the resurrection is not an essential, first-order issue. The Jesus event is infinitely valid and important whether or not he was raised from the dead on the third day.

Everyday resurrection

It seems ironic in that while the Church struggles to understand the resurrection at the end of Jesus' life, it often ignores the repeated instances of resurrection *during* Jesus' earthly life. When you think about it, the gospel accounts are packed with resurrection stories and events.

The defiled and rejected leper, physically embraced and healed by Jesus, is given new life; the woman with the haemorrhage, ostracised and degraded by the religious laws of the day, is reborn; the man lost in a nightmare of mental instability who thinks he is possessed by a legion of demons returns to the world of the living; while the prodigal son is still far off, the grieving father glimpses the child he thought was dead and runs to greet him; the prayer we call the Lord's Prayer brings a powerful vision of life and hope, destroying isolation and despair. These and many other events speak of resurrection: for the poor and, in a strange way, resurrection for the rich as well.

Just as Jesus works tirelessly to bring the good news of God's love and justice to the oppressed, so too he works to jolt and shake and challenge the rich into new life. He says to the rich young man (Mark 10:21) go and sell all that you have and give it to the poor. How is that going to help the poor, apart from donating a few thousand tins of baked beans via a food bank? It isn't. The problem is structural. What causes much of the world's poverty is plain and simple greed. A greed driven by insecurity. A greed that is rapidly poisoning the planet and threatening to destroy the human race.

One rich man giving his possessions to the poor is not the answer. So why does Jesus tell the rich man to give away all his possessions? Because they are a barrier to *him* receiving life. They imprison him and Jesus is a liberator. What Jesus is offering him is not a sharp financial shock but resurrection. The rich man did not have the courage to accept the challenge and he went away sorrowful, but not before Jesus had embraced him. It says Jesus hugged him. It seems Jesus did not look on the rich man with contempt, but with love and understanding. He embraced him – just as he had embraced the leper when he healed him.

As frequently happens in the Gospels, there is a mirror image of the story of the rich young man. Remember the rich tax collector who climbed the tree to see Jesus pass by? Come down from the tree, shouted Jesus (Luke 19:5). I must come to your house and eat with you tonight. Amazed and delighted, the much-hated Zacchaeus scrambled down and rushed off to start cooking.

At the feast, Zacchaeus stood up and said, to everyone's surprise: if I have robbed or swindled anybody I will pay them back four times over. There was huge applause and amazement because Zacchaeus was known to be very tight-fisted when it came to money. Was his grand gesture going to change the world or the poor? No, but it changed Zacchaeus – and Jesus knew it. Today salvation has come to this house, he says. And what is salvation but resurrection? Life in the place of death.

The Church tends to pass lightly over these incidental resurrection encounters with the homeless Jesus. Encounters in which the poor are raised up to new life and the rich and powerful are brought down from their thrones, as the Magnificat says.

But the rich are not cast out. Instead, loved by God and frequently embraced by Jesus, they are sent away empty *in order that,* being empty and dead to a world of wealth and privilege, they may be filled with life.

One of the essential characteristics of this is equality. The idea that all humanity is loved by God and that no person is more important in God's sight than another. The leper in Mark chapter 1, verse 40, is equally as important as the rich young man. Both are offered the gift of resurrection. One receives it but the other cannot do that and goes away sorrowful. At least for the time being.

As we begin to realise that the gospel accounts are full of resurrection stories and as we approach the horror of the crucifixion, we see this resurrection dynamic continuing right up until the last. In words we cannot entirely rely on, but whose power overwhelms us, Jesus prays: 'Father, forgive them, for they know not what they do.' (And, if they do know, then forgive them anyway?) What is that but resurrection?

Then there is the split second in Luke's Gospel where the resurrection word is spoken, not by Jesus but *to* him. When the man crucified alongside him says: 'Jesus, remember me when you come into your kingdom.' Did he actually say 'when' and not if? The high voltage charge of that word crackles with resurrection life, even at the moment of death.

But who might have been courageous and close enough to hear that word? Attentive and astute enough to register and remember it? People whose presence near the foot of the cross was a matter of indifference to the Romans. People who did not matter. People who were invisible. A few unimportant women.

Did the resurrection really happen? Despite our understandable cynicism and doubt, there is a sense in which the resurrection couldn't have *not* happened. The gospel accounts are, as we have seen, full of resurrection. It's as though the life-giving love of God is travelling so fast through the Gospels that when it comes to the crucifixion it can't stop. It just goes hurtling on into what the Church calls Easter.

7

St Paul and the dead cat

I once managed to upset a whole roomful of people by uttering a single word. Not that it was entirely my fault. The incident happened at the start of a Christian conference. The organisers had planned an unusual ice-breaker to help the participants get to know each other. The idea was that each of us was to say which person in the Bible we hated most.

Judas Iscariot, naturally, came in for a lot of stick. He was followed by people like Cain, Satan, the chief priests, various scribes and Pharisees. Even the snake got a dishonourable mention. At each answer there were nods of polite agreement.

When it got to my turn I said the person I hated most was Paul. There was a deathly silence. The temperature in the room seemed to drop. For a few moments I must admit I quite enjoyed the notoriety, but later I felt guilty as I realised what I had said was not absolutely true.

I definitely have serious reservations about Paul but I don't hate him. He was probably saying and doing what seemed right to him and being faithful to God as far as he was able. Which, in truth, is all that any of us can do.

But there is still a big problem with Paul. Basically, I believe Jesus got it absolutely right about God but Paul got it significantly wrong. And, more importantly, the things that Paul got wrong get in the way of the things

Jesus got right. For many people, the power of Paul's writing effectively blocks the message of Jesus.

A journalist might see in this a hint of the 'dead cat' dynamic: a dramatic intervention that distracts attention from a controversial agenda item at a meeting, as if someone had thrown a dead cat onto the table. Suddenly everyone is talking about the cat and forgets the main item of business.

Why might anyone want to do that? Perhaps because the original agenda item threatens the vested interests of powerful people. Or, in the case of the Church, people simply found the Jesus agenda too alarming?

But you can't kill the story by arguing that Jesus was wrong. As we have seen, 'good news for the poor' comes from Isaiah, one of the major Old Testament prophets. You simply can't ignore both Jesus and the prophets and get away with it. There would have to be a diversion – and, whether by accident or design, St Paul provides it.

Did he intend that to happen? Probably not. Is Paul to blame? Not necessarily, but what he wrote and its extensive presence in the Bible meant the dead cat effect was inevitable.

Changing sides

The story of Paul is dramatic. In his early days, it seems, Paul was a religious extremist. He was among those who hunted down Christians and persecuted them. The hope was that by inflicting fear and violence on the followers of Jesus, the new Christian sect would disappear.

But all this changed when, according to the Acts of the Apostles, Paul was on his way to Damascus. Without warning there came a blinding light and Paul said he heard the voice of the risen Jesus asking why he was persecuting the Christians. The Church calls this the conversion of St Paul, but Paul wasn't converted from Judaism to Christianity. He remained a Jew, but one convinced that the Jewish hope and expectation of a messiah had come to pass in Jesus.

For Paul, Jesus wasn't the negation of Judaism or its replacement, but its fulfilment. That was a thought so powerful it overshadowed everything else. From then on, Paul became a passionate ambassador for the risen Christ. His new-found mission in life was to bring people, Jews and gentiles, to a life-saving faith in the risen Lord.

Inspired by this vision, Paul spent the rest of his life travelling to important places like Athens, Corinth, Thessalonica and Galatia to spread what he called 'his' gospel. He became known as the apostle to the gentiles, with the emphasis on the definite article.

Paul had boundless energy and a high degree of theological training. Intellectually he was awesome. He wrote powerful letters to the churches he himself had founded and, although he had never been there, a massively complex theological letter to the church in Rome.

The church in Rome? Where did that come from? If Paul was 'the' apostle to the gentile world, who was it that founded the church in Rome – the centre of the known world, possibly most important city there had ever been? Not Paul.

Undaunted by this, the Church holds Paul in extremely high esteem, not least because it says that if it were not for him, there would be no Christianity. Paul, it is said, created the worldwide Church. Without him, Christianity would have remained a tiny Palestinian sect that would have quickly disappeared.

So where did the church in Rome come from if it wasn't Paul? And why hadn't he gone there to help in its formation? In fact, why didn't he start from there? With excellent communication channels to the whole of the Empire, Rome would have been the obvious launch pad for his work and Paul knew the importance of working strategically. This matters because, for the Church, his uniqueness gives added importance to his presence in the Bible – and the diversionary effect of his epistles.

All that glitters

The Rome question is particularly puzzling when you remember that Paul, unlike Jesus, seems to have been very fond of cities. Indeed, he is described by Luke as 'a citizen of no mean city' – meaning his birthplace, Tarsus.

Jesus, on the other hand, avoided cities. Rural peasants had a very low opinion of cities, and Jesus was more than likely a peasant in terms of social standing. Cities were built by the wealthy as secure locations for their palatial residences and became the nerve centre for their exercise of power, oppression and injustice. Money gravitated to the cities. To the poor, cities meant greed and corruption.

Only when his ministry was coming to its grim climax did Jesus finally go to Jerusalem. But, far from regarding it as holy, he said it was the city that murdered the prophets.

This, in turn, leads us to notice other differences between the scholarly Paul and the vagrant preacher from Galilee. Paul visited towns and cities, creating fixed church communities. Jesus, on the other hand, visited villages and seemingly created nothing more tangible than a vision of hope and justice.

Unlike Paul the builder, Jesus didn't seem keen on building anything. In the story of the Transfiguration on the mountain top, the three disciples propose building shelters for Jesus, Moses and Elijah. But Jesus never hangs around in one place for long, and the shelters never got built. Jesus was on the move again.

To be sure, Jesus was interested in one building: the Temple in Jerusalem. But his concern was not to praise it but to destroy it. Unlike the militant zealots, he wasn't a reformer. He was enough of a drinker to know you couldn't rehabilitate old wineskins. And for Jesus, the Temple had gone sour. As we have seen, the place had become a focus for oppression, not sustaining but destroying the lives of the vulnerable. A den of rich thieves who robbed the poor.

Was Jesus aware of Paul's existence? Almost certainly not. But what is astounding is that Paul, writing twenty or thirty years later, appears to know nothing and care nothing about Jesus, apart from his death and resurrection. Remarkably he shows almost no interest in what Jesus might have said and done, or in why Jesus was born at all, other than to save us from our sins. What mattered to Paul was that Jesus (a) was the Messiah, (b) that he humbly and obediently accepted death on the cross and (c) that he rose from the dead – a mighty act that heralded the deliverance of all believers.

But, if the divine purpose was simply that Jesus should be a perfect and innocent sacrifice that redeems us from sin, why hadn't God allowed King Herod to succeed in his plan to murder the infant Jesus thirty years earlier?

Unasked questions

Reading the epistles, Paul doesn't seem to consider the earthly work of Jesus significant. In all the times that Paul met and spoke with the other Christians who had known Jesus, did he never ask questions about the man they followed? Did Paul never say: 'Tell me about Jesus.'? Did he never ask: 'What was Jesus really like? What did he do and say?' His letters show little knowledge or interest in Jesus the human being or in his teaching.

Maybe Paul thought that Jesus hadn't understood his own earthly ministry. That he only received the full and divine knowledge of his life's purpose after he had been raised from the dead. To be sure, there are points of overlap with Jesus but these are few and far between. Jesus is passionately concerned about bringing good news to the poor and oppressed. Paul also shows concern for those experiencing poverty. But, for him it was not the mass of humanity starving in the rural areas of first-century Palestine and beyond, it was the tiny group of impoverished Christians living in Jerusalem to whom he wanted to send aid.

Paul seems to turn a blind eye to the regime of terror inflicted on the poor by the Romans and the indigenous leadership in Palestine. And there are clues to why that might have been so. Firstly, according to the Acts of the Apostles, Paul, as well as being a Jew, was also a Roman citizen. If that was so then he was a member of a high status group. Paul wrote letters – and writing was an elite activity. Only the children of the well-off received formal education, and Paul had that in spades. He employed a scribe to pen his epistles. Scribes and writing materials cost money.

He was wealthy enough to embark on numerous sea voyages – and presumably these did not come cheap. As part of the social and economic elite he may have seen poverty from a very different angle to that of the low status, itinerant Jesus. While Jesus was constantly challenging the economic and social injustice that oppressed the poor in first-century Palestine, Paul seems not to notice. He accepted the existence of slavery as a normal fact of life, as did most of the rich and powerful who benefited from it.

Those on the receiving end of slavery did not necessarily see it that way, as evidenced by events like the revolt of Spartacus, many years before. But it was to Paul and not Spartacus or Jesus to whom the Church looked for guidance when the slave trade developed in the colonial expansion of the sixteenth century.

And so the suffering and exploitation has continued to the present day with sexual, domestic and economic slavery: from people in the crowded sweatshops of the global south to those forced to work in our car wash facilities or pimped for sex on our streets. The confiscation of passports and the threat of physical violence or even death may have replaced the iron manacles that held slaves captive in the past, but the inhumanity has never ended.

The Body of Christ?

One of the many problems with Paul is not just that he wrote complex theological letters, but what he said in them. For example, in his first letter to the church in the cosmopolitan and apparently immoral city of Corinth, he uses the image of the human body. All was not well with that church and Paul was writing to urge unity and order.

Christian believers, he says, are like the limbs and organs of the human body. They are all different but all have their necessary functions. None is greater and more important than another. They are united in a single body and the head of this body of faith is Jesus Christ. Within that body all are equal, whether male or female, Jew or Greek, slave or free. It's a great image and central to the Church's self-understanding. The problem is that it's not true – and that presents major problems for us today.

But what can possibly be wrong with the image of the body with its equally important parts interacting in an orderly and coherent manner? Firstly, its different parts are simply not equal. Your brain is more important than your left leg. You can live without a hand or arm or kidney, but you would struggle without your heart or lungs. You can manage without your eyes but not without your arteries. Indeed, if it is infected by meningitis bacteria, the body will often sacrifice external limbs such as fingers and toes, arms and legs as blood circulation is withdrawn from the extremities to protect vital internal organs in its literally self-centred struggle for survival.

Secondly, Paul knew that not all parts of the Church were equal. When he lists the various Christian activities or functions he places the apostles first (1 Corinthians 12:28). Paul was an apostle, and, outside Palestine, he was *the* apostle.

Thirdly, and perhaps most importantly, the body is an organism enclosed in an envelope of skin. It is separate from other organisms with the boundary between the internal organs and the external world rigorously protected. What comes in and goes out are strictly controlled. Penetration by an external agency must be prevented, except in the case of food and acceptable sexual activity. The body is an image of unity to Christian insiders, but to others it is an image of separation and insularity. Two things Jesus didn't like.

The Exodus problem

It is traditionally agreed that the Exodus was a very good thing. To the Hebrews it was the seminal event in which God intervened to rescue his chosen people from their captivity in Egypt and lead them to a new life in a promised land. But the Exodus narrative also contains elements of profound negativity.

Whether or not the Hebrew people were delivered out of slavery in Egypt as a matter of historical fact is not certain, but it is the manner of that apparent deliverance that is important. As we have seen, the blood of lambs was used to mark the Hebrews out as separate from the Egyptians

After a long sojourn in the wilderness, they reached their destination. But the land of Canaan was not empty and the Hebrews, determined to remain separate, eventually defeated the Canaanites in battle. The land was now theirs, apparently by God's gift. That made their deliverance from slavery permanent. Both the promise and the land were essential.

But, if we think about it, there are further negative aspects to the Exodus story. Not least what it says about God. Looking back on the deliverance narrative, God does not choose to put the Egyptians into a deep sleep and allow the Hebrews to escape. Instead there is anger and retribution. God kills all of their firstborn children. So how do we square the mass murder of innocent children with the idea of a loving God whose nature, we are told, is always to have mercy?

Down the centuries the Exodus story has stood as a powerful symbol of God's desire to free those living under oppression. People living under systems of injustice in Latin and South America still see it as a narrative giving hope of liberation and justice.

But the Exodus narrative has also contributed to injustice and oppression. The idea that the Hebrews were specially chosen by God inevitably sets them apart from other people. And that separation is one of distance and inequality. Of polarity. The Hebrew scriptures tell us that the Canaanites were defeated in battle because they worshipped a false god and committed abominable acts.

It is not surprising the Hebrews were hostile to other religions. Lying at the eastern end of the Mediterranean, the land in which they settled was a corridor between Egypt to the south and Syria to the north, used by a mixture of ethnic groups with differing religious beliefs.

The Hebrews believed that other religions were false and that a protective distance must be maintained to avoid pollution of their worship of God. This was particularly so in the case of the Canaanite god Baal.

A similar dynamic was almost certainly operating when it came to Paul. As we have seen, the Romans were keen to co-opt indigenous tribal leaders to assist in the smooth running of conquered territories. But they were also willing to co-opt local tribal deities into their ever-expanding pantheon of gods. One more god made little difference to the Romans and it kept the local tribal leaders happy. But this accommodating pluralism would not have made Paul happy and he would have been all the more determined to defend the purity of his own belief system.

Are you in or out?

The trouble is that this sense of difference and superiority has created unintended consequences. Being the 'chosen' people implies that others are not chosen: that God differentiates between 'his' people and those who are not his people. And there can be no greater inequality and differentiation than that.

This polarity of acceptance and rejection, however, is inconsistent with love and therefore cannot be reconciled with the concept of God as loving and just. Love affirms life and purpose. Life and purpose in its highest form is to share in the creative activity of God.

This inclusion/exclusion dynamic reappears in the Gospels where Jesus repeatedly comes into conflict with the religious leaders. Jesus is essentially inclusive, accepting people stigmatised by others as being sinful and unclean. The more orthodox religious leaders, however, are instinctively exclusive. They are reaching back into the ancient tradition of the chosen. Jesus meanwhile is looking to the Old Testament prophets with their demand for inclusivity, love and justice, even for the alien.

But Paul saw the emerging Church as the transformed and fulfilled Israel. Consequently it, too, needed to be united, not just internally, but united in distinction to external groups and religions. Barriers had to be maintained. Converts were welcome, but their incorporation was conditional on a belief in Jesus as the Risen Lord.

The problem is that this doesn't seem to fit with the Jesus we meet in the Gospels. Born into the Jewish community and living in a land invaded, exploited and in religious terms polluted by a pagan power, Jesus might have been expected to be very keen on barriers and the idea of ritual purity.

But it was just the opposite. He constantly challenges the protective purity code, he breaks the cohesive religious law and shares food with so-called sinners, deadbeats and dropouts. He embraces the unclean and never once asks to see their ID cards. Jesus is inclusive in his relationships and in his understanding of God.

Key point of difference: Paul does body. Jesus does yeast. Body is safe. We stick together behind our barricades when facing external threats. We go out into the world to win converts but only when those converts are willing to join our body of believers and be washed clean in the water of baptism. Anyone other than that is wicked, unclean and ultimately damned.

In contrast, yeast is all over the place. Yeast disappears and then bubbles up again. It lifts the lump of dough into something light, nourishing and edible. It changes fruit juice into wine.

Paul lives his stern theology of the body and gives us a new religion, characterised by orderliness and obedience to his teaching. He urges his churches to live quiet lives of gentleness, patience, kindness and conformity to the civil authorities. They, he says, are the divinely appointed agencies of peace and stability and must be obeyed.

For Paul, or others who may have written in his name, the state was the mirror image of the human body, guaranteeing protection and guarding against dysfunctional chaos. Exactly the argument used by tyrants to justify oppression. Just what Jesus spent his life challenging.

Instead, Jesus comes across as the black sheep of the family. He lives a disorderly life of boundary-free subversive liberation. Despite all the suffering and pain, this life somehow manages to be bursting with laughter. And he seems to suggest that this reflects the nature and character of God.

But Paul gives us a very different image of God, and that is no laughing matter. So we need to focus on some further aspects of Paul's personality and his mode of operating.

8

Paul the fighter

There's a story about Field Marshall Montgomery who commanded the British Army during the Second World War. Monty, as he was nicknamed, was a small man but had a very pugnacious manner. 'I'm a fighter,' he famously boasted. 'I'll fight anybody.'

But what might be useful in a general is not necessarily ideal in an apostle. Maybe Paul saw himself as a commander: he certainly saw himself as fighting a war against evil. There is a lot of energy in Paul, but also anger and violence.

As we have seen, in his younger years his loyalty to the religion of his ancestors had been extreme – surpassing all others. Psychologists might call it a pathological attachment. He was apparently present at the murder of the first Christian martyr, Stephen, and applauded the killing. Paul admits that he persecuted the Church savagely and ravaged it because it threatened his own religion (Galatians 1:13). Where did that anger come from and, more importantly, where did it go?

In one of his letters, he speaks of sin itself being defeated and led captive in a ceremonial procession called a triumph. But a triumph was an occasion when a defeated ruler was led in chains in front of jeering crowds before being humiliated and brutally executed. It was an image of extreme violence and retribution.

In Romans 12:20 Paul speaks of giving food to an enemy when he is hungry, but the latent anger shows in the final words – thus you will heap coals of fire on his head. And, vengeance is mine, says the Lord.

Paul, like Montgomery, seems willing to pick a fight with anybody. He has a row with the disorderly Corinthians, homosexuals, the 'stupid' Galatians, Peter, Barnabas, the 'dogs' and 'spies' in the Church who disagree with him, and just about anyone who he thinks does not recognise Jesus as the Messiah. If anyone has no love for the Lord, let him be accursed, he says in the closing lines of his first letter to the church at Corinth.

Paul seems to love a fight: as long as he wins. And winning mattered to Paul. In the context of a world that offered a multiplicity of 'gods' that was not surprising. In 2 Corinthians 9:24-27 he speaks of punishing his own body like an athlete who trains hard in order to win a race. Paul may have felt himself to be competing with other belief systems, but finding salvation in the love of God is never a race that favours the fittest. And history teaches us that inflicting pain as a way to holiness is not a good idea.

The big one

His letter to the church in Rome is the first epistle we encounter in the New Testament and for many people it's a difficult, almost impenetrable document. But even the most simple minded of us can pick up on alarming Pauline concepts such as the 'wrath' of God. After its formal introduction, still on page one, the letter proper begins with the two words: Divine retribution.

There are not many words in the Bible more different to Abba. Where is the much deserved wrath and retribution in Jesus' story of the prodigal son, we might ask? Where is the wrath and retribution in the idea that God loved the world so much that he sent his son to show us his true nature? Wrath and retribution are about judgment and punishment, but Jesus does not judge or punish.

The God of St Paul counts the cost. The God of Jesus doesn't seem to be greatly concerned about accountancy. Are we to forgive as many as seven times, the disciples ask Jesus as they try to work out how love works. Not seven times but seventy times seven times, says Jesus, smiling. Forgive endlessly. Just keep doing it.

And while he's telling them to do the impossible, he's turning on its head the law of an eye for an eye and a tooth for a tooth. Specifically, he is also using the Old Testament story of an embittered man called Lamech, who swore that his revenge for an offence against him would be 'seventy times seven' worse than the crime committed.

Jesus sits at table eating and drinking with us in easy companionship, but Paul approaches us with the hammer of fear. Fear of sin. Fear of damnation. Fear of what Paul sees as the wicked world in which no one is righteous, no one seeks for God. No one does good. There is an enemy and it is invisible he says. Our warfare is with unseen spiritual powers. Be afraid.

Fear, it is said, hinders rational thought. Politicians use it to achieve and retain control. We have a common enemy, they say. We are under threat. For Hitler it was the socialists and the Jews. For Stalin it was the capitalist system and revisionists in his own party. For the people in the West today the external threat is the Russians, the Chinese, cyber terrorists, Middle Eastern terrorists or some nebulous axis of evil. Bogey man politics. Bogey man theology.

Meanwhile Jesus urges the poor and the oppressed not to be afraid, despite the enormity of the forces of oppression ranged against them. And *never* be afraid of God.

As a child

Perhaps, if he had ever heard him speak, Paul would have thought Jesus naïve, simplistic, possibly childlike. Which reminds us of the difference between Paul and Jesus when it came to children. Jesus, as we have seen, took a child and placed it in the middle of the crowd. Then he told the people they must become 'like a child' if they wanted to enter God's kingdom. He was speaking about hierarchy and power, though he may also have been indicating the exuberant and dynamic nature of God's kingdom.

But when it comes to Paul, things are very different. If Jesus was a bit of a kid at heart, Paul was very much a grown-up. When I was a child I spoke like a child, I thought like a child. But when I became a man I gave up childish ways, Paul says sternly in his first letter to the Corinthians (1 Corinthians 13:11).

Maybe Paul had never met a child, spoken to a child or listened to a child. Maybe he never had children of his own, otherwise he would have discovered that there is a lot going on in a child's head. Wonder, creativity, tenderness, imagination, wisdom, laughter. Picasso said that he spent all his adult life trying to learn how to draw like a child. What was it that Paul regarded as childish, I wonder?

One morning my six-year-old daughter stopped eating her cornflakes for a moment to ask: 'Daddy, what's life for?' That seemed like a very grown-up question to her bemused father. There is a world of difference between being childish and being childlike.

Looking back, there seems little love in Paul, but plenty of expediency. Is there warmth or gratitude? Does Paul have love for Jesus or is Jesus simply the believer's passport to eternal life? The believer's 'stay out of hell' card.

Do we sense the touch of God's love in Paul's writing? Did Paul even experience the love of God? References to love in 1 Corinthians 13 and Philippians chapter 2 are well known. However these do not sit well, textually, with the rest of the two epistles and it is not possible to know whether these words are by Paul himself or later insertions by others.[1]

---

1   See *Paul's Letters from Prison* by J. H Houlden, page 68, and *The First Epistle to the Corinthians* by C. K. Barrett, pages 297 and 299.

Jesus tells us to speak with God using the intimate and trusting word Abba. But when Paul uses the word Abba, it is in relation to the inheritance a child receives when it grows into adulthood (Romans 8:17).

So, too, Paul's own hopes for the future seem to be about acquisition – and transaction. *My* desire is to depart this earth and be with Christ, he says (Philippians 1:23). And for other believers? We share Christ's suffering *in order to* share his glory (Romans 8:17). Really? Not: we share Christ's suffering because we want to share in his love for the world? And count it a privilege to do so.

It is as though, for Paul, Jesus is the gatekeeper between the wicked world and the kingdom of heaven. But a gate implies a barrier. Separation. And, for many, exclusion. And here we are back to Exodus and the chosen people.

Paul says that *if* you believe that God raised Jesus from the dead *and* that he is Lord, *and* confess it with your lips, *then* you will be saved (Romans 10:9). But the Jesus we meet in the Gospels has reassuringly lower standards. He is theologically untidy, accused of being a glutton and a drunkard, a friend of sinners, breaker of the law, a blasphemer and shameless, according to those whose vested interests he threatened. The kingdom is among *you*, he tells all and sundry, publican and prostitute, clean and unclean. No barriers. No gates. Not exactly Paul's sort of boy.

But how can Jesus not be Paul's sort of boy if he had been granted a one-to-one interview with the Risen

Lord on the road to Damascus? Did something get lost in translation?

A mind in turmoil?

Is it beyond the bounds of possibility that Paul's guilt at the persecution of Christians was catching up with him? Did his anger, previously directed at the early Church, morph into anger directed at what he saw as an evil and corrupt world?

He speaks of 'his' gospel and 'Christ in me' as though he and the Risen Christ have almost become one entity. It is as if he is the self-appointed ambassador, broker, and spokesman for the Risen Lord. Model your lives on me, he urges his readers. On him rather than on Jesus. Take *me* as your example, he says (1 Corinthians 4:16 and 11:1).

Is this a pride that needs to excel? Or is it a mind in turmoil? Perhaps there is a hint of narcissism in Paul. Who knows, maybe his bitter condemnation of homosexuality was an unconscious reaction to his own unacknowledged sexuality.

His influence on the Church today is so powerful that we do need to consider the factors that might have been the driver for his writing, and Paul, it seems clear, was a driven man. This may not have been a characteristic deliberately chosen by him, but it nevertheless creates problems for us. His complex writings, bursting with energy, throw up endless opportunities for theological argument and debate that, in turn, use up vast amounts of time and energy.

Meanwhile Jesus, with an apparent lightness of touch, manages to condense his message into three words. Love your neighbour. (Words that remind me of my brash claim to have hated Paul. On reflection, I must admit I now find myself having some sympathy for this brilliant, damaged man. I may not like him or agree with him, but he is my brother. My neighbour.)

The trouble is 'love your neighbour' are not the first three words you necessarily associate with the institutional Church. Nor are they the first three words you read when you open the Bible. And that is a big problem, for us and for our planet, as we shall discover.

9

The great betrayal

It must have been quite a fight. It's clear from the surviving documents that Paul and the leaders of the Church in Jerusalem were divided over a number of issues, including what food it was acceptable to eat and whether male Christians needed to be circumcised like the Jews.

What also seems clear is that Paul, the theological brawler, won the fight. We know this because his letters, or some of them, were included in the New Testament but hardly anything from his opponents survived. The victor always gets to write the history.

But there was another fight going on at the same time. As we have seen, Paul's views differ radically from those of Jesus in a number of ways and there came a point early on when the Church had to decide between the two. And, once again, in the physical absence of Jesus, Paul seems to have been the winner.

The first disciples were living in turbulent times. Apart from the economic and social oppression experienced by the majority of the population of first-century Palestine, there was increasing political unrest. Jesus had been crucified for sedition because he was thought to have been a threat to the stability of the state.

As followers of Jesus it was not at all clear whether a similar fate might await them if they continued with the subversive agenda Jesus had proclaimed. Prudent people might think it wise in those circumstances to lie low. The demand of Jesus that they take up their cross and follow him in the struggle for justice and the love of God had never been an attractive proposition and, following the actual crucifixion, had probably become even less inviting.

To ordinary people living in fear of arrest, the package Paul was offering must have seemed like manna from heaven. Paul's image of the Christian community as the body of Christ, with Jesus as its head, is simple but powerful and must have given the early Christians a real sense of who they were.

As we have seen, a body is an insular organism, separate from other organisms. The physical body finds safety in its insularity, and the early Church found, if not safety, at least reassurance in its unity and cohesion. While Jesus had called for engagement with the world, the image of the body encouraged a distancing from the world. Come out and be separated from the world, urges Paul. Be pure. No unclean thing shall you touch. You are the new Temple of God: a temple that must be pure and holy (2 Corinthians 6:16, 17).

Before long there was a rite of initiation into the Christian community. You must be baptised into Christ's body, the Church told potential converts. Be washed clean of your sins. Come and be saved.

How tempting it must have been to forget Jesus in the gutter of life getting his hands dirty from the touch of lepers and sinners, saying follow me and never mind all this purity stuff. Jesus telling the ordinary people they were to be like yeast permeating the world to challenge the powerful in their oppression of the poor.

Lifeboat practice

It is said that several of the disciples of Jesus had been fishermen and that, in an earlier life, Paul was a tent maker. But what might fishing and tents have in common? Quite a lot, it seems, when you think about it.

How did Peter and the others go about catching fish? They used a boat. What does a boat do? It separates you from the threatening sea. It keeps you from drowning. You stay safe and dry on the inside, while the dangerous waves stay on the outside. The boat is a refuge, a place of safety – so long as the hull remains intact. No wonder the Church developed the idea of the ship of faith, floating on seas of sinfulness and chaos in the world. The Church as the lifeboat of the world, rescuing sinners.

Who in those turbulent days would have felt like reminding Peter that Jesus once invited him to get out of a boat and walk to him over the water? Peter was safe in the boat and wasn't going anywhere: until Jesus yelled at him to jump over the side of the damn boat and come to him.

One of the demands that Jesus made of his disciples was that they follow him: not just spiritually in their hearts, but with their feet, walking from village to village, dirty, hungry and thirsty. Later the disciples reminded Jesus they had left everything, their homes and their families, to be with him on what must have seemed a very dangerous expedition. And, to be fair, they had a point.

But what about Paul and his tents? What is a tent? A shelter from adversity. From the sun in hot, dry weather and from the rain and snow in winter. A refuge. Like an upside-down boat, it's a place in which you can separate yourself from the threatening elements. A place of relative safety. A place where a family might live.

Paul reassures his converts by telling them they are like a family. In fact, they are a family: the new family of Abraham. A family of faith, a family united in a common ancestry. Anyone who has seen Shakespeare's play *Romeo and Juliet*, however, will know that families have boundaries. Paul is keen on boundaries: Jesus less so. In fact not at all.

Remember the incident when the family of Jesus turned up to try to persuade him to abandon his foolhardy mission (Mark 3:32). No wonder they were worried about him: his work was not only endangering him but, by association, them as well. Your family are outside wanting to see you, the disciples told Jesus. And what was his reply? Those who do the will of God are my family.

And who does that? Anyone who shows love for their neighbour. Anyone who shows love is, in that act of loving, being my kin. Not just the Jew but also the hated Samaritan. Anyone. But 'anyone' is not a family word. It does not denote purity or faith or formal kinship. It isn't a boat word or a tent word: it's a no-boundaries word.

Paul's message appears essentially transactional. The message of Jesus, however, is relational. You are loved. No matter what you do or who you are, you are loved. And that love is life. In loving others you celebrate and affirm that life-giving love. No boundaries. No conditions.

Paul is reassuringly exclusive: Jesus is worryingly inclusive. Paul asks you to believe, but Jesus hardly seems to care what you believe. It's what you do that counts. Think about the story of the house built on rock (Matthew 7:24).

The disciples came to Jesus and said: we saw someone healing in your name. So what? says Jesus. Who cares? Those who aren't against us are for us. In first-century Palestine, that must have sounded alarmingly casual. What people needed, or thought they needed, was to be safe. And Jesus wasn't big on that.

With zealot groups becoming increasingly active and stirring up all sorts of trouble, and with the Romans getting increasingly angry in response, there was likely to be trouble ahead. Who would you go for in that situation: Jesus or Paul?

So, not only does Paul provide the early Church with the ultimate comfort blanket of incorporation into the Body of Christ, he depoliticises both Jesus and the cross. No longer is the cross a politically dangerous event: it is now a spiritual matter. For Paul the focus is on cleansing from sin, the affirmation of faith and membership of the Church that becomes the new and fulfilled Israel. The family of Abraham.

(Ironically the new Christian sect did encounter persecution but this was largely because it refused to recognise the divinity of Caesar, not because it opposed the injustice and suffering imposed by the powerful upon the poor.)

The Eucharist

From the earliest days the Eucharist, or Holy Communion, became the central liturgical focus of the Church. Key to that tradition are the reported words of Jesus: 'this is my body' in reference to the breaking and sharing of the bread at the Last Supper. But this creates a further complexity. Not only is the fellowship of believers the Body of Christ but, it seems, the bread at the Eucharist is also the body of Christ.

It is likely that the 'Last Supper' was the culmination of the fellowship meals Jesus had shared with his followers and many others. By all accounts, those meals had been open to all and an important expression of Jesus' barrier-free ministry. But in all four Gospels it is claimed or implied that the only guests were the 'twelve' disciples. A select male group.

As the centuries roll by, this exclusivity creates two further areas of segregation. Firstly, that only committed Christians, the baptised, should be allowed to share in the Eucharist and, secondly, the belief that among the followers of Jesus in first-century Palestine, there had been a core group of men with elite status.

Regardless of whether that hierarchical model can be consistent with the radical equality that Jesus called for, that is the pattern that the historical Church has replicated. It might be worth noting at this point that some biblical scholars take the controversial view that the idea of the twelve disciples may well have been a much later invention of the Church, created to represent the twelve tribes of a new Israel.

Influenced by the pattern of worship in the Jerusalem Temple, the clergy have emerged as a group within the Church with significantly different degrees of hierarchical status, ascending from lowly lay folk via deacons, priests, canons, archdeacons, deans, bishops, archbishops and cardinals up to the Papacy itself.

And beyond the Pope? Far above us all, sitting in glory at the right hand of God the Father, in the blessed company of saints and martyrs, is the Risen Christ. You have only to look at how this is pictured in art, particularly of the medieval period, to see how that worked. Much of that art was commissioned, and no doubt influenced, by the wealthy princes of the Church. They were paying the piper, and they were certainly choosing the music.

There must have been many in the early Church who rejoiced at that powerful hierarchical imagery. The challenging egalitarianism of Jesus had been replaced with a far more palatable scenario. His message of justice and love for the vulnerable and oppressed had been superseded by a ladder of sanctity, leading from the sinful world below to the very presence of God.

The betrayal

One of the most poignant images in the gospel accounts is the betrayal of Jesus by Judas Iscariot (Mark 14:44). The Church has always held Judas Iscariot up as the epitome of evil. The devious friend who became the ultimate enemy. But Judas has been very useful for Christians. No matter how bad we are and no matter what terrible things we do, we reassure ourselves that we can never be as evil as him.

Strangely the Church never seems to have asked what would have happened if Judas had not betrayed Jesus. He would almost certainly have been arrested and crucified anyway. So does it matter how the arrest came about?

The irony is that, year by year in the passion narratives, the Church remembers the events of Jesus' betrayal and execution, yet it forgets its own betrayal of Jesus – which may be far more significant and destructive.

Judas, we are told, betrayed Jesus with a kiss. The institutional Church has been betraying Jesus ever since with the cold kiss of religion by which it domesticates and distorts the gospel. Judas betrayed Jesus actively: the Church betrays him by its passivity. It delights in the saying 'Be still and know that I am God' and ignores the fact that Jesus was active and often angry. An anger that was a driver in the work of love.

But with his followers, it seems, it was not so. Instead we find Paul telling his churches to be obedient to the civic authorities, because those in power have been placed there by God. And the Church has followed that pattern into the present day. At times when the world needed the crucial intervention of the Church to avert disaster, it has repeatedly failed the world.

If the Church had been true to Jesus there might well have been no Adolf Hitler and no Joseph Stalin. If the Church had done its job there might have been no German or Italian fascism and no Russian communism.

Grinding poverty for the masses under the Tsar in Holy Mother Russia had led to the Communist revolution of 1917 and the subsequent rise of Stalin. As a result, tens of millions died. People like Tolstoy had spoken out against the poverty and injustice suffered by the people but the Tsar was the head of the Russian Orthodox Church – and the Church was silent.

During the First World War the Bishop of London, Winnington-Ingram, spent a lot of time stoking up hatred against Germany. The Prime Minister, Asquith, was so appalled that he accused the bishop of preaching 'jingoism of the shallowest kind'. But it was just that sort of ongoing inflammatory jingoism that helped create the Nazis. After the war the Treaty of Versailles imposed crippling and unjust conditions on Germany, many of whose population faced starvation as a result.

Even as the treaty was being drawn up there were widespread warnings that it would trigger a terrible retribution but urged on by the Foreign Secretary, a prominent Christian layman, and the influential right-wing Press, it went ahead. In all this the Church remained silent. The treaty was duly signed. There was smouldering resentment among the German people.

Hitler was on hand to fan the flames, and the monster of fascism was born.

Time and time again, whether in Europe, Russia, Africa or Latin and South America, the Church as an institution has colluded with injustice, supporting violent oppression and dictatorial regimes.

In Britain today the Church often values the rich more highly than the poor. It has frequently acted as a compliant chaplain to governments intent on damaging and destroying tens of thousands of lives across the country. In a time of extreme poverty and injustice, only a handful of Anglican bishops out of more than 100 effectively challenged the status quo. Among the rest, those who do care about poverty and injustice did little more than express polite concern and disquiet and the hope that something might be done.

The same has been true in the Catholic Church. While Pope Francis has pleaded with the world on behalf of the poor, the poor planet and the poor Jesus, the majority of the church leadership has stayed resolutely silent. And to remain silent in the face of injustice is to collude with oppression.

Never mind about global warming and its threat to the human race, the Church frets about dwindling attendance figures, commits itself to ineffective campaigns of so-called evangelism and agonises over who might be sleeping with whom.

Of course, down the centuries, there have been and are many examples of Christian individuals and church projects that have 'served' the poor and marginalised.

But the emphasis has been and continues to be on a pastoral response to the symptoms rather than a more demanding engagement with the root causes of injustice. Food banks are an example of this. The parable of the Good Samaritan has been grievously misinterpreted in this respect.

The superficial 'sticking plaster' approach favoured by many churches is not just a disastrous betrayal of the poor and marginalised, it is a profound betrayal of Jesus. By demonstrating that it does not care about the core issues that mattered to him, the Church is, in effect, saying he does not matter. And, if Jesus is the incarnation of the nature and purpose of God, as the Church teaches, then it is in danger of communicating the message that the will of God does not matter. And that is serious.

10

The Bible and the banana skin

When it comes to the Bible, the Church is divided roughly into two groups: those who think it is the literal word of God in its entirety, and those who believe it contains the word of God, along with other material. The problem for the first, conservative, group is that different parts of the Bible contradict each other: it's not consistent. Even Jesus contradicts earlier parts of the Bible.

Thinking back to our last chapter and the idea of forgiveness, we saw the Old Testament teaching that an offence should be met with a payment: an eye taken in retribution for an eye destroyed by an attacker. However, Jesus tells us to forgive and, indeed, to love our enemy. But, if the Bible is God's word given to us verbatim, surely it must be consistent?

Meanwhile the second, more liberal, group of Christians say the Bible is not the literal word of God, and that some parts of it should and must have priority over others. This invites the accusation that the liberals simply pick out the parts of the Bible that suit their own point of view and ignore the bits that don't.

The answer to this charge involves a banana. Think about it. Many people take a banana to work for their lunch, but nobody eats the whole banana. The skin and stalk are part of the fruit but, no matter how much they like bananas, no one eats the outside bits, even though they are organically part of the fruit. They pick and choose which parts to eat.

Liberal Christians believe the same applies to the Bible. The Bible has within it the word of God but comes with a lot of secondary material. And quite a few errors. The trouble is, it's often hard to tell which parts are essential and which form the outer layers.

A journalist might point out that newspapers only print the news they think is important, so why can't the Church do the same? After all, most Christians believe the crucial parts of the Bible are the Gospels.

But, say the theological experts, you can't understand Jesus without the Old Testament. Is that true? Do we need to read and understand 1,000 pages of scripture before we even get to Jesus?

Reality check: God has been trying to communicate with humanity for several thousand years and the Church has been trying to spread the good news of Jesus for two thousand of those years. And between them they produce a book, the contents of which are frequently self-contradictory and whose main character, Jesus, does not appear until page 1,065.

To Christians the Bible may be a greatly revered book: to others it's a communications disaster. What matters is not that we revere a holy book but that we engage seriously with what Jesus said and did in the context in which he lived.

Putting it crudely, I'm tempted to say that I don't have time for the Old Testament or St Paul. It's taken me most of the last fifty years to begin to understand the first word of the Lord's Prayer. Three score years and ten simply is not enough time to get our brains round everything that is in the Bible. Nor do we need to.

Meanwhile global warming is rushing towards us like an incoming tsunami, and unless we learn to love our neighbour and the planet, there will not be much time left for us to read anything.

So what role does the Old Testament have? Resisting my temptation to ignore it all, perhaps we should put it respectfully to one side, at least for the time being. Instead of starting with the Old Testament and working our way forward to Jesus, maybe we should start with Jesus and then, when necessary, refer back to the Old Testament for clarification and explanation. Use the Old Testament as a valuable resource like Google, rather than essential preliminary reading.

Some people will no doubt be unhappy with this suggestion. Most churchgoers are familiar with passages from both the Old and New Testament being read out at services. But the unspoken assumption from that pattern of worship is that the Old and New are of equal importance. My argument is that they are not. Jesus is like the pearl in the oyster: you don't need to know that pearls come from oysters in order to appreciate the beauty of the pearl.

Jesus is the human expression of the nature and purpose of God. The incarnate Word of God, to use the technical term. Thankfully, the surviving Jesus material is relatively brief and, in the main, not very difficult to understand.

Except that . . .

A sinking feeling

Hard on the heels of the alarming realisation that the Bible sometimes contradicts itself, there comes an even more profound shock.

When I went to theological college I was told that the Jesus sections in the New Testament are not necessarily all real Jesus. Some of them are probably made up. I was horrified, but I should not have been. How many times do reports in newspapers and on the broadcast media contain fake news and political bias?

Local media outlets are usually fairly accurate in the material they print but the national media is notorious for political bias and its reluctance to let the facts spoil a good story. National journalists don't distort the news every day of the week. However, they are aware of the political stance of the media outlet they work for, and what sort of emphasis would be most appreciated. The proprietor may not take an hour by hour interest in what their newspapers print, but they will have made their views and preferences very clear to the editor. Newspaper proprietors are rich and powerful people with vested interests they are keen to protect and promote.

I knew all that. But I had never realised it might also apply to the writers of the Gospels or the people who decided which documents should be included in the Bible and which excluded. Nor had I realised that the Gospels were written down in the form we have them many years after the events described.

It felt as though the ground had given way under my feet. Was there anything about Jesus that was rock solid, apart from the fact that he lived and died? That might sound overdramatic, but some Bible 'experts' argue that there isn't. They point out that Jesus never left any written notes or sermons, and the people who told stories about him are not reliable in the sense of their ability to give us accurate historical facts.

Therefore, the experts argue, we can know virtually nothing of the earthly Jesus. All the more reason, they say, to focus on Paul. He was literate, wrote his thoughts down, and that documentation has largely survived intact. (In fact the experts now tell us that some of the later 'Pauline' letters are not by the apostle at all, but the basic argument holds good.) Over time, however, I began to realise that all is not lost when it comes to Jesus. You just need to do a bit of detective work.

Time for a time line

How then might our investigation begin? By reviewing the available material. The gospel accounts were written down years after Jesus was executed, so where did the gospel writers get their information? And how reliable could that data be?

To come anywhere near an answer it's useful to draw up a time line. Look at it this way:

04CE	Probable date of birth of Jesus
30CE	Probable start of his controversial public ministry
31CE	People talking about Jesus, remembering his words
33CE	Jesus executed by Romans, assisted by Temple leadership
45CE	Paul travelling, writing his epistles
55CE	Mark probably gathering material for his Gospel
55CE	Paul executed by the Romans
63CE+	Mark writing his Gospel
65CE+	Mark's Gospel completed
75CE+	Matthew and Luke's Gospels written
100CE+	John's Gospel written

It is not suggested that these dates are accurate, but they give us an idea of the time scale we are talking about.[2]

So, if Mark was writing his Gospel in the months or years leading up to 65CE, what information was available to him? Were any eye-witnesses still around?

---

2   An extended version of the time line appears at the back of this book.

As far as we can tell, if you survived the first five years of life as a child in first-century Palestine, your life expectancy was about 35 to 40 years. As now, it may be that women lived longer than men.

So what women do we know about? The women at the tomb. All four Gospels say that one of the women who went to the tomb of Jesus after the Crucifixion was Mary Magdalene. She seems to be significant. The first three Gospels list the women who went to the tomb, and in all three accounts Mary is named first. If she had been born around 15CE, she would have been in her mid-teens when Jesus started out on his public ministry. Did this young teenager join his group then? Was she one of the girls who had been ejected from the family home to find work as a domestic servant or, failing that, survive by begging or prostitution?

Mary would have been 18 when Jesus was executed. When St Mark was gathering material for his Gospel, around 60CE, she would have been 45: getting on in years but quite possibly still alive. Did Mark actually speak to her and people like her? Nor should we exclude younger children who encountered Jesus. Would they have remembered anything? Maybe so.

I have vivid memories of my own childhood, including things people said and did. Once, at the age of four, I was taken to a children's party. After a particularly interactive game, I was found sitting at the bottom of the stairs crying. I was upset because the girls wanted to kiss me. A kindly man came to my rescue and I clearly remember his prophetic words: 'Lad, there'll come a time when you'll cry because girls don't want to kiss you.' He was so right. Some years later I joined the Cubs. I never got past the introductory 'tenderfoot' stage but I can still recite the Cub Promise word for word.

Kids are impressionable and impressions stick. A child of seven or eight could easily remember some of the sayings and actions of Jesus thirty years later when Mark was putting together his Gospel. Mark may be the only gospel writer to have direct contact with people who saw and heard Jesus. But how reliable would those accounts be?

In an era when few people could write and even fewer could afford writing materials, stories were passed on by word of mouth. Obviously, if this was just casual gossip, then a message would be hopelessly corrupted. Strangely, Jesus' itinerant ministry may have helped to imprint his sayings and deeds on people's minds. Had he lived among them for long periods, what he said might have got lost in the numerous day-to-day conversations. But his brief visits were, by their nature, unusual and therefore memorable.

Similarly after his crucifixion and ascension, those who had known him would naturally have begun to reminisce about his words and deeds. When someone we love dies, our natural reaction is to recall their lives and tell each other stories about shared experiences and memorable sayings. We look at photos and obituaries are sometimes written to recall the person who has died.

Fortunately the ancient oral tradition of remembering significant sayings and events seems to have been more disciplined than that. As a result, much of the material in at least the first three Gospels may have been passed on with considerable accuracy. Paul, probably writing round about 45-55CE, speaks of 'the tradition' of the Eucharist that he had received. That means the oral or written accounts that were available to him.

Twenty years or so after Mark wrote his Gospel, Matthew and Luke were probably gathering material for theirs. By comparing the texts, we can see they incorporate a large amount of Mark's material into their Gospels but they also appear to have had access to another, earlier, common source.

Short and sweet

Admittedly, mistakes often creep in to a document in the editing process and writers who use other people's material are sometimes tempted to improve on the original. The result is that, while it would be reassuring to think the gospel writers always recorded the words of Jesus faithfully and accurately, we cannot be sure they did. In reality, they didn't.

So the question is: how do we sort out the real Jesus from the additional material incorporated by the gospel writers? Fortunately, recent research has given us a clue. The thinking is that Jesus typically taught by using challenging sayings. He sometimes used outrageous and ridiculous images – like a pompous man walking around unaware he has a plank of wood stuck in his eye, or the idea of people trying to push a bad-tempered camel through the eye of a needle.

In contrast to our received impression of Jesus as a person of placid and calm piety, it seems he teased and joked with the crowds – doing anything that would help his words to be remembered. In fact he used sound bites. Talking to people with no way of recording his words except by memory, it would make sense to use brief, punchy sayings.

That being so, it is quite likely that the short stories and sayings we find scattered through the Gospels are more reliable bedrock Jesus than the longer speeches sometimes attributed to him. For example, it is easy to remember a simple, controversial sentence such as: 'The last shall be first.' Compare those five words to the long seventeenth chapter of John's Gospel which is a single quotation of more than 500 words.

The chances are that this also applied to his parables. But what about the long parables, especially those that appear to be in two parts? How tempting it must have been for Luke to hear the story of the return of the prodigal son and the father's outpouring of unconditional love, then add the second part about the older son. The second part is, it seems, a veiled criticism of the Jews who refused to recognise and accept Jesus. But, if the parable is about the love of God, the second part is unnecessary. It may have been added for good measure, but it clouds communication of the key issue.

Similarly, in the story of the Good Samaritan, the real Jesus story may have ended with the Samaritan stopping and helping the man who had fallen among thieves. The impact of the story is that the priest and Levite, wishing to protect their ritual purity, passed by on the other side. But, controversially, and therefore memorably, it was the despised Samaritan who risked his life to help the wounded man.

The second section of Luke's story about what happened when they got to the inn is irrelevant. It would have given Jesus' listeners unnecessary material to remember and process. As indeed it does for us. But, if it was unnecessary, would Jesus have included it?

We saw a similar editorial process in the story of the labourers in the vineyard (Matthew 20:1-16). Matthew introduces the parable with the words 'the kingdom of heaven is like . . .' The trouble is it's not like that at all. As we have discovered, the story is about greed, exploitation and revenge directed at the vulnerable by the powerful. Jesus isn't describing the kingdom of heaven, he is describing a living hell imposed on the poor by the rich.

Whatever Matthew's intentions, the result of the editorial process is often to weaken, domesticate and even subvert the message of Jesus. In doing so it provides a less demanding challenge to his later disciples, as we shall see.

A useful guide

So how might we begin to find the 'true' Jesus? One way might be to ask:

- Is the statement in the style of Jesus: terse, controversial, pithy, gritty and humorous?

- Content: does the story communicate the love and justice of God?

- Consistency: how does its imagery fit with Jesus' critique of the hierarchical Onion?

- Does the core message continue into a non-essential second section, and should we treat that additional material with suspicion?

Strangely we may also glimpse a clue to Jesus' personal background in all this, though we cannot be sure of it.

When writers are creating stories, they often draw on their own experience. In fact they frequently incorporate aspects of their own personality into their characters. Sometimes a character in a story might be the author in disguise. Might Jesus have done this? Was the speck of dust in the eye a sharp fragment of sawdust? Did Jesus have first-hand experience of that? And of how heavy a plank of wood can be? Had his father really been a carpenter?

Did Jesus see himself as the Good Samaritan: rejected by the religious establishment and kneeling in the gutter alongside the vulnerable and outcast? Was Jesus the prodigal son who walked away from his birth family and seemingly brought disgrace on them? Was Jesus the good shepherd, turning his back on those in the religious fold to find the lost and the rejected? Was Jesus the argumentative labourer in the vineyard who refused to bow down to the exploitation of the powerful, even when it meant banishment and death? In the story of the talents, did Jesus see himself as the rebellious servant? The one who refused the temptation to collude with the money-making machinations of the rich? The one who dared challenge the powerful oppressor to his face – and was destroyed for doing so?

Rough diamonds

In this chapter we have been concentrating on the first three Gospels of Matthew, Mark and Luke. These can easily be compared to each other in both structure and content. However, the fourth Gospel, attributed to an unknown figure called John, is significantly different.

If the first three Gospels include an untidy patchwork of stories and sayings, John's Gospel is, for some people, like a magnificent cathedral. It is a wonderful commentary on the gospel narrative rather than an attempt at an objective account. Its long and complex chapters fit well with formal institutional religion and are typical of a style used by historians of the period. But, textually, they don't appear to have much in common with the Jesus of the first three Gospels.

In fact, along with St Paul, the fourth Gospel seems to begin the process of burying the real Jesus under a mountain of words. Often those words are majestic, but sometimes they are misleading. What, for example, are we to make of the sublime statement in John 3:16 that God so loved the world that he gave his only son . . .? Standing alone, that seems to express the essence of God's unconditional love.

The problem is that the rest of the sentence imposes a draconian exclusivity: that whoever believes in him (the son) should not perish but have eternal life. So what happens to those who, for whatever reason, do *not believe* in him? The logic of the statement is that they consign themselves to perish – to death.

Even those who never knew the name of Jesus? Even those for whom the beloved son has been obscured by an inward-looking Church? Even those of no faith who self-evidently live out the love and justice we see in Jesus and yet do not fulfil the Church-imposed criterion of faith? A requirement notably lacking in the earlier gospel accounts of Jesus.

Then there is the question of anti-Semitism. The first three Gospels almost entirely avoid using the term 'the Jews' when talking about those who opposed Jesus. In contrast, that term is used constantly in the fourth Gospel – with catastrophic consequences.

As we have seen, the powerful indigenous elite who colluded with the Romans in opposing Jesus were obviously Jewish. But Jesus and his followers were also Jews. Using the term as St John does in the fourth

Gospel, the way is paved for the *whole* Jewish race being held forever responsible for the death of Jesus.

The consequences of that hardly need spelling out. There have been a number of holocausts in modern times other than that of World War Two, such as the genocide in the Belgian Congo and the virtual extermination of the indigenous peoples of North America. Even more have died in some of those events than were murdered in the Nazi atrocity. No group has a monopoly on suffering. However, there is a focused evil intent that marks out the Nazi outrage as being particularly appalling, coming as it did after centuries of discrimination against the Jewish people.

How far is all that from the words of Jesus, urging us to love our neighbour and forgive those we regard as our enemy? The Church believes the words of Jesus from the cross: 'Father forgive . . .' are authentic. How then can it have colluded with centuries of anti-Semitism? How can it so easily have lost sight of that core gospel message?

Giant Haystacks

Once upon a time there was a wrestler called Giant Haystacks. As I remember, he was very large, rather untidy and extremely difficult to get hold of. Which is basically where we are with the Bible.

The scriptures can feel like a theological haystack and finding the real Jesus is like looking for the proverbial needle. At first it seems so simple. The Jesus material is in the Gospels but as we have seen, the Gospels are crushed in the vice-like grip of the Old Testament on one side, with the Acts of the Apostles and the heavy-duty letters of Paul on the other.

The Old Testament raises the expectation of a nation-saving messiah, but Jesus turns out to be absolutely not the sort of warrior messiah they were expecting. Paul meanwhile says almost nothing about Jesus, other than he died and was raised on the third day. How strange that the letters of Paul tell us so little about the life of Jesus and yet the Gospels, written down years later, appear to tell us so much. After being beaten into submission by the heavyweight Paul, were the gospel writers staging a return match a few years later?

The process of collecting, recording and editing the accounts of Jesus' life seems to have extended, distorted and softened the message of the carpenter from Galilee. But, when we remember that writing was an elite activity of the educated and relatively wealthy in the Roman world in which the voices of the poor were silent, it is astounding that *any* of the radical Jesus survives.

Did the gospel writers not realise what they were revealing? That just under the surface of innocent-sounding stories, there was a subversive, politically explosive dynamic operating? Was even more controversial material lost or deliberately edited out by men with their own vested interests? Surely it is legitimate to ask how much *more* challenging Jesus was in real life?

Giving thanks

We should be immensely grateful for those anonymous people who handed on the stories of Jesus to Mark and the other gospel writers, especially given the extreme political turmoil in which they lived. In 70CE, after years of rebellion, the Romans finally lost patience with the Jews and destroyed the Temple. The impact of that event must have been catastrophic. But the dangerous, turbulent years leading up to that disaster were the ones in which the heart of the New Testament was being created.

In all that turmoil and within those scatted Christian communities, who was remembering? Possibly the people to whom his words meant the most. The words of Jesus seemingly didn't matter to Paul, but they mattered to the poor of first-century Palestine. And, as we have seen, the poorest of the poor were the women. Women whose voices were not heard in public. Prevented from speaking, they probably listened all the more intently to the man who showed them respect.

Perhaps it was women like those who risked their lives bringing aromatic spices to the tomb who were largely responsible for the outpouring of precious memory that makes up the gospel.

The Bible begins with the disastrous imagery of the Garden of Eden in which a tyrannical male God condemns humanity in general, and women in particular, to eternal pain and suffering. It is a story. Myth clothed in mystery. It seems hardly anyone treated it as literal truth until Paul came along. But the imagery and impact are real.

After centuries of foreign occupation and oppression, there arose the hope of a messiah. A king. A warrior who would deliver the nation. A hierarchical male image of violence and conquest. But it was the *wrong* hope. Tempting though it might have been, Jesus did not claim to be, or try to be, that messiah. To have done so would have been to create exactly the wrong expectation.

Maybe it was the female followers of Jesus, hardly mentioned in the Gospels, who, listening and remembering, redeemed the cumbersome and confusing Bible. And, in that way, played a crucial role in the birth of a new understanding of God. Perhaps they still do.

11

Getting it wrong: the disciples

As we begin this chapter, the year is on the turn. The days are getting shorter and the nights drawing in as summer gives way to autumn. The seeds I planted in the allotment that germinated and then survived attacks by slugs, caterpillars and pigeons have finally produced a crop. Not being a gifted gardener, I am constantly surprised that anything grows.

Thinking back to the some of the gospel stories, I wonder whether Jesus was also surprised when the unexpected happened. Like the time a woman is said to have gate-crashed a meal and poured expensive perfumed oil onto his hair in a wordless act of love and solidarity. There was great indignation from the other guests that so much money had been wasted.

Who was the woman? Was she so wealthy that she could have afforded such a lavish gesture? Probably not. But how could such a gift have come from the poor? Someone condemned as being of ill repute: a worthless prostitute? How might that incident have come about? Had she told her friends what she was planning to do? Knowing how Jesus had fought for justice for the marginalised, did they all share the cost?

Did it start with one person's crazy idea but then develop into a corporate expression of solidarity? An action that threw the greed of the rich back in their faces with a symbolic act of generosity so very typical of the poor? Was Jesus surprised at the woman's sudden and inappropriate appearance at the meal? Was he surprised when he realised the perfume was so expensive that its fragrance filled the whole house? Was he surprised when he realised the woman had either robbed a bank or that others had given their much-needed money to share in that exquisite gesture of love? They may well have needed the money for their own survival, and that would have made the act infinitely more precious. They didn't need to do it.

But did Jesus need it to happen? At the moment when things were moving to a disastrous climax in his life and death was not far away, did he need someone to give something back to him? A wonderful, tangible, unforgettable gesture of costly love? Did the fragrance of the oil linger with him for days, as the aroma of expensive perfume tends to do? In his mind as well as on his body. Could he still sense it when it came to his arrest and torture? Perhaps even to the horror of the execution. Semi-conscious from his brutal beating and now nailed to a cross, did it stay with him as a final blessing?

When the men had deserted him and only the women disciples stood near as he died, was he surprised? Surprised that those who had made the loudest protestations of loyalty had disappeared, seeking their own safety, but those who had said little but given much were with him at the end? Jesus had sown seeds, but what would be the harvest? Did he glimpse a future of justice and equality brought about by such courageous women? Were they his true disciples?

A man's world

If there had been no resurrection on the third day Jesus would at least have been spared what came next.

It is one of the mysteries of the gospel that the women, who had been largely invisible in the Jesus narrative, unexpectedly come into clear focus at the crucifixion. As we have seen, it was the women who endangered themselves by being with him at the cross, who risked their own lives by daring to go to the tomb on the third day, and who were the first messengers of resurrection to the other disciples.

But then, as now, it was a man's world. And men would very quickly reassert their power and control over any women who happened to be around. And their control of what became the Church.

But the problem is even more deep-seated than that. Think of the word tribe. Usually we regard tribes as having to do with primitive societies but the 'tribe effect' operates in all sorts of situations. And not always for the best. Tribes unite their members but they also divide the wider society. Just as they include, they also exclude.

If I identify as being black, I am not white. If I say I am male, I am not of the female tribe. If I say I am rich, then I am self-identifying as not being poor. To be included in our social tribe gives us a sense of security and affirmation. Humans are social creatures. We derive our humanity from social interaction. The danger of being excluded from our tribe can create anxiety or fear.

There seems to be a dynamic therefore that encourages tribe membership and the strengthening of that tribe. But to strengthen one group often involves weakening another. This dynamic was demonstrated by an experiment carried out in the late sixties in a school in the United States. In the days following the assassination of Martin Luther King, a teacher called Jane Elliott decided to explore racism with her class of eight year olds. Her method was alarming but effective.

Elliott gave the all-white class some startling information. People with blue eyes, she said, were superior to people with brown eyes. The class was then divided into the two groups. The children with blue eyes were given privileges and told they were good and bright. They were allowed to sit at the front. But those with brown eyes were told they were inferior and unintelligent. They were made to sit at the back. Within minutes, the behaviour of the children changed. Those with blue eyes became assertive and aggressive, while those with brown eyes became passive and withdrawn.

The following morning there was another surprise. Elliott shocked the children even more by telling them she had lied to them the previous day. In fact, she said, it was the children with brown eyes who were superior to those with blue eyes. Remarkably, the children's behaviour patterns reversed as the new information was internalised. In the discussion that eventually followed, the children realised that eye colour was of no significance when it came to value and, by extension, they were beginning to learn that skin colour was also immaterial.

Years later one of the blue-eyed children, now in his sixties, admitted that within minutes of the experiment starting he had been 'tremendously evil to my (brown-eyed) friends, going out of my way to pick on them'. He added: 'I was a perfect little Nazi.' Why had the children behaved in that way? Because they had been told by a powerful authority figure that the other group was of lower value.

The nightmare

On a larger scale, that process is called propaganda. In 1930s Germany, people suffering the grossly punitive effects of the treaty of Versailles, were exposed to Nazi propaganda. The result was that they turned on their inoffensive Jewish and homosexual friends, neighbours and others, creating the nightmare of the Holocaust.

In the 1990s in former Yugoslavia, Christian Serbs massacred thousands of Bosnian Muslims who, only months before, had been their friends and neighbours. The people committing these atrocities were not psychopaths, they were ordinary people among whom a latent tribalism had been triggered.

It may be that we have a similar dynamic emerging from the writings of St Paul. For him the Christian tribe is made up of the saved and righteous, in contrast to the pagan outsider. Paul's image of the Body is the Christian tribe, in distinction to other tribes. But Paul does not simply say the pagan tribe is different. As we have seen, he stigmatises it as evil and corrupt, deserving of the wrath of God (Romans 1:18 to end).

That distinction increased group solidarity within the 'faithful' and 'righteous' Christian tribe and raised its sense of status as the chosen ones of God. Hierarchy, which Jesus so powerfully opposed, was being reintroduced. The process ran as follows: God chose Abraham; the Hebrews are the chosen seed of Abraham; Jesus is the fulfilment of Judaism; Christian believers are the family of Abraham. For family, read tribe.

Ironically the Church, which values its unity as the body of Christ, has been torn by tribal disunity from its earliest days. Peter and the other disciples didn't always listen to Jesus. Instead, while he was still here on earth, they lobbied as individuals for their own hierarchical status, each wanting to sit next to Jesus in places of honour in the future kingdom.

After the resurrection Paul argued furiously with Peter and the Jerusalem leadership. As the years went by there was conflict as various so-called heretics questioned church orthodoxy. Later the eastern and western churches split; the western church divided again at the Reformation when Christians burned each other at the stake, and the reformed churches fragmented into a number of protestant groups. And all this time the Church has claimed that it was being guided by the Holy Spirit. For Christian denomination, read tribe.

Down the centuries the tribal Church has inflicted and colluded in extreme violence on other groups.

These ranged from the crusades against the Muslims to colonial wars and acts of genocide against the indigenous people of North America, India and Africa in which tens of millions were killed.

In the sixteenth century, the protestant reformer Luther sided with the aristocracy who slaughtered up to 300,000 people in the Peasants' Revolt in Germany. His argument was that, at all costs, civil order must be maintained. St Paul might have approved but there was not much by way of good news for the poor.

The Son of Man

The trouble is that we don't see this tribalism in Jesus. More than eighty times in the Gospels he refers to himself as the Son of Man. The translation of this term, from both the Aramaic and the Hebrew, is simply: a person. A non-tribal human. Jesus is also typically non-tribal with others. In fact he seems to be against the idea of tribes in general.

He challenged the tribal inequality that was created by the rich for the rich. But this did not mean creating a tribe of the poor. Contrary to the Old Testament words of the Magnificat, in which the rich are sent away empty, Jesus embraces the rich. He greets the rich young man with open arms, treating him with inclusive love, not with judgmental contempt.

He shares meals with the rich even when they are known to be oppressors of the poor. We saw this in the story of Zacchaeus, the man who climbed the tree. Zacchaeus was not sent away: he received life. What happened to his tribal identity? It simply dissolved. The Magnificat warns that the rich will be put down from their high places and the poor exalted: an exchange of tribal fortunes. But Jesus doesn't do tribes.

Border control

But, if Jesus didn't do tribes, how is it possible that he gave St Peter the 'keys of the kingdom' (Matthew 16:19)? Keys are about barriers, separation and control. They lock and unlock doors. They deny admission, or allow it. A judgment has to be made before the key is turned, and that judgment is an exercise of power.

There are few images more tribal than keys. And, we might think, few people less appropriate to handle keys than Peter. But not only does Peter get the instruments of control, he is also given the power to judge who may and may not enter.

Does this commission really come from Jesus? The one who said: 'judge not'? How did those first disciples get it so wrong? They seem to have ignored or forgotten what Jesus was working to achieve. 'I have been anointed to bring good news to the poor,' he said. A dangerous statement.

Did the disciples hear those words? Did Jesus not repeat that agenda in the same or similar terms a hundred times when people asked: what are you doing? Did the disciples not understand that he was bringing good news to the poor and vulnerable every day of the three years he was with them? Did they listen to a word he said? Would they have listened if God had spoken to them directly? Did they listen when, it seems, God did exactly that?

What vital words get overlooked in the story of the Transfiguration (Mark 9:2-9)? Run the film slowly. Jesus takes Peter, James and John to a high place. Suddenly his robes start to shine with a brilliant light. The disciples have a vision of the glory of God reflected in or refracted through Jesus. Alongside Jesus are two other figures from the Old Testament.

There is a voice. It is God, saying, 'This is my beloved son.' But something is missing from that brief summary. God speaks directly to the disciples and gives them a command. What does God say to them? Three words, which are included in all of the first three Gospels: '*Listen* to him.' Listen to what Jesus is saying to you. Divine commands don't come much clearer than that. But while Jesus was on earth alongside them, the one thing the male disciples seem seldom to have done was to listen to him.

The new tribe

Why do we say that? Because, after the resurrection, instead of continuing Jesus' subversive, grass roots work for justice and equality those disciples started a new tribe, with themselves as its leaders.

Jesus, the embodiment and carrier of the justice message of God, is replaced by the risen (and now silent) Jesus. The resurrection has become the message. And the more the institutional Church gazes up adoringly at the ascended Christ in glory, the less it seems to take seriously why he came among us. The new church tribe is not the borderless, dispersed and political 'justice and the love of God' movement of Jesus, acting like yeast in the world. Instead it quickly morphed into a religious 'believe and be saved from hell' tribe.

Why might that happen have happened? Perhaps because it's a lot easier to maintain and control a tribe if it has a clear, achievable goal. For the disciples that goal was to proclaim to the world that:

- Jesus is the Risen Lord;

- that gift of eternal life is obtained by personal belief in him;

- that the alternative is the wrath of God.

A cynic might say that is a far more attractive package to sell than the idea that they should continue what Jesus did: risking their lives challenging injustice. Had self-preservation replaced self-giving?

Walking the talk

We've been using the word disciple, but what does that term actually mean? And what did it mean to the early Church? In the world of ancient Greece a disciple was someone who came and sat at the feet of a great teacher. And stayed in that place, listening and learning.

Jesus, however, didn't stay in one place: he was always on the move. Were his followers learning? Apparently so, but not always by listening. The fact that they followed Jesus physically meant that they were exposed to different situations. They were also participating in action and learning from that experience. At least twice in the gospel accounts, Jesus is described sending his disciples out into the towns and villages to proclaim the good news.

The Church has taken this to indicate that an elite group were being marked out for leadership. But the opposite might well be true. It's quite possible that Jesus, realising that verbal education was not having much effect on some of the disciples, sent them out to learn the hard way.

He told them not to take money, or luggage, or shoes or coats. They were to have no possessions that would need protecting and which would indicate status. They were to be poor, as the people they would encounter were poor. Perhaps Jesus hoped they might learn from their challenging experience.

The great sell-out?

How far the new church tribe was from the radical Jesus movement, we might guess from the Acts of the Apostles (2:46). There we read that every day the disciples were worshipping in the Temple. That might have been normal practice for many people, but these were the followers of the man who had only recently demanded the physical destruction of the Temple and condemned the injustice and oppression that emanated from it.

The Temple, as we have seen, colluded with the Roman invaders and was the focus of economic exploitation. It was a trading arrangement that would have been jealously guarded by the powerful. The Temple was the last place on earth disciples of Jesus would have frequented: unless they were in denial about their allegiance to him and their earlier participation in his subversive movement.

Did the Temple authorities not arrest them for being collaborators with the seditious Jesus of Nazareth? Or were Peter's denials carried over into the post-resurrection Church? If they were challenged by the Temple guards, did they shrug and say: 'We did not know him.'? Is what we read in Acts true? And does it matter?

The first part of Acts is all about Peter. Then, halfway through, Peter disappears and the second part of the narrative is all about Paul. There is no mention of the radical Jesus agenda. Did Luke, who recorded the parables and deliberately included the provocative Magnificat in his Gospel, really go on to write the relatively uncontroversial Acts of the Apostles that reflects none of Jesus' dangerous social agenda?

Jesus was executed for opposing injustice and refusing to back down. That radical stand cost him his life. It was a moment of supreme commitment to God. But, just as the Romans took away his life, it seems the disciples are now in danger of taking away his message and his purpose. There can be few more effective closure strategies than to transform the centre of betrayal and opposition back into a sanctuary for daily prayer.

Effectively this is saying, the Jesus on earth project is over and we are back to religion as normal. Together, the Acts and the epistles effectively shut down the Jesus story.

The great commandment of Jesus is to love God with all our heart and our neighbour as an integral part of that love. In contrast, the self-proclaimed 'great commandment' of the Church is to go out into the world and make disciples. But does that mean disciples as in activists engaging with the Jesus agenda to oppose injustice and bring good news to the poor, or does it mean trying to persuade more people to join the newly-formed religious tribe?

The real temptations

In the gospel stories of the temptations in the wilderness (Luke 4:1-13) Jesus is tempted by the Devil. First he is tempted to turn stones into bread. Then by being offered dominion over all the nations of the world. Thirdly, he is tempted to put God to the test by saving him from death. Was Jesus really tempted in this way? Does that narrative reflect reality? Thinking back to the crucifixion, it may well have done.

What is certain is that, from the beginning, the Church faced very similar temptations and gave in to all of them. If Peter denied Jesus three times after his arrest, this was the most devastating and long-lasting fourth denial. In a few short years the Jesus project went from the liberation of the poor to salvation for the religious.

The rejected son of man was replaced with the prestigious hierarchy of the institutional Church. The name of the game changed from subversive servanthood to power and control over people's lives: earthly and eternal.

The tribal barriers Jesus took so much trouble to demolish were being rebuilt. Deliberately or by accident, the Jesus problem had been contained. The work of the disciple was no longer about love and justice but political conformity and self-preservation. Job done.

12

What is God like?

It is the central argument of this book that the Church, either by accident or design, has buried the real Jesus under centuries of dogma and tradition. What he did and said has, for most people, been lost under a blanket of religion. The trouble is that what the Church has done to Jesus, it has also done to God. The barrier that separates us from the real Jesus is also in danger of separating us from our Maker.

We have begun to explore why the Church might have done this and, to be fair, the challenge of Jesus is an alarming one. Loving God and our neighbour might well end in our own violent death. To 'take up your cross' is not a call to religious abstinence or about enduring a difficult colleague at work. It is a challenge to confront, in non-violent ways, a powerful political machine whose capitalist vested interests we are threatening.

But not only does the Church try to avoid these political and economic confrontations, it also degrades and obscures the meaning of a vital word: love. The Church treats love as an abstract noun but, for God, it is an extremely active verb. Love means much more than having a kindly and sympathetic disposition towards another person. It is a social and therefore political activity.

We are urged to love our neighbour through our actions, no matter who that person might be. Whether we happen to like that person or not: to love even those we regard as our enemy. That activity of love consists in working for the well-being and fulfilment of the other person. It means opposing anything that damages them. Which is precisely why Jesus was executed.

Jesus worked for the well-being and fulfilment of others, particularly those who were vulnerable and being damaged by the oppression of the rich and powerful. And that included marginalised women. But, as we have seen, he did not simply love the poor and hate the rich. He may have found the exploitative actions of the rich hateful, in that they oppressed the poor but he loved the wealthy and actively worked for their well-being.

When the rich young man came seeking eternal life, instead of rejecting him as an enemy of the poor, Jesus showed him how his longing could be fulfilled. It may be that the key to that unexpected response comes from way back in Luke's Gospel where Jesus is reading in the synagogue. As we have seen in chapter 2, the passage of scripture he turns to is Isaiah chapter 61.

But, as Jesus reads those familiar words, he appears to miss something out. And what he leaves out is significant. Identifying himself with the reading, Jesus says he has been sent by God: to proclaim good news to the poor, recovery of sight to the blind, freedom for those whose lives are broken, the debt cancellation of the Year of the Lord . . .

Then, it seems, he stops. In the middle of the sentence. Jesus is only partway through a verse of the scriptures. The Isaiah reading continues with the words: . . . and the day of vengeance of our God. The idea of the vengeance of God might have been acceptable to Isaiah writing 500 years earlier, but not with Jesus. And that is surprising.

As we know, first-century Palestine was occupied and exploited by the Romans, and its people betrayed by the Temple hierarchy and rich landowners. You might think that would be exactly the time for 'the vengeance of the Lord' to kick in. But, according to Luke, Jesus leaves those words unspoken. If that is the case, then everyone in the room would have noticed. It was a famous passage of scripture and they knew how it should end.

Was Jesus careless or was that omission intentional? In fact, crucial. Perhaps he was saying this has been your understanding of God, but I am telling you something radically different. Not simply that God loves humanity, but that God's love is unconditional. And, if it is unconditional, it cannot be consistent with revenge.

The father did not take revenge on the prodigal son. His love was without condition. When he took him in his arms, the father did not know why the boy had returned. He did not care about that. The father in the parable represents God. Jesus, however, is describing the parental love we would normally associate with a mother. But that is not the image of God the Church has projected over the last two thousand years.

The hardliners

Beginning with Paul, however, we get a return to the alternative non-Jesus narrative of a wrathful God. In Paul, the powerful imagery of Adam's fall from grace is held up, not as an ancient myth but as a present and immediate reality. It is a reality in which the image of an angry and vengeful God is reactivated. God's imagined reaction to Eve's moment of apparent disobedience is not forgiveness but brutal condemnation.

Three hundred years later, this punitive dynamic was given further and lasting impetus by St Augustine with his hardline theology of original sin. All are born in sin and remain in sin until redeemed by God's grace in baptism. But where did Augustine's abrasive thinking come from? What made him the way he was? Part of the answer was clearly St Paul, but there was also the pear tree.

It happened this way: Augustine was born in North Africa in 354CE in a town surrounded by hills. Those fixed and immovable hills influenced his thinking. He liked stability. The house he lived in as a child had a mosaic floor. Augustine was fascinated by the way the small coloured stones fitted together. Their fixed patterns created order out of chaos. That image stuck with him: he liked order.

Once he went on a sea voyage. The sea kept moving about: he hated that. As a teenager he went round in a gang. One day they raided a garden and stole pears from a tree. Not one or two but a whole heap of them.

The pears, however, were too unripe to eat, so the boys threw them all away. Augustine was consumed by guilt over that stupid prank, and the guilt stayed with him.

Why had they done such a senseless thing? Because in a group it is easy to egg one another on in the excitement of the moment. It reinforces group solidarity and gives you the reassuring feeling you are one of the gang. Security. It seems his view of original sin was made powerfully immediate and personal by that wanton act. We are, by our nature, flawed from birth he concluded.

Later, as a young man, Augustine had a concubine and, by her, a child. Such an arrangement was sanctioned by the Church, but as his Christian calling developed he and the woman became estranged. In fact, it appears Augustine abandoned her. He had enjoyed sex but found it emotionally disturbing. Now he had an increasing feeling of guilt about his past.

Finally, on top of everything, Rome was invaded. In 410CE the Visigoths captured the city. Alaric, the Visigoth leader, was an Arian Christian. Bitter divisions between Catholics and Arians over the nature of Christ's divinity led to persecution, torture and murder. Tribal conflict at its worst.

On the surface Catholic Rome had seemed as solid as a rock but underneath there had been a disturbing dynamic at work. We assume that by the time of Augustine Rome was divided into Christians and Jews on the one hand and godless pagans on the other.

However, it appears that the 'accommodating pluralism' of the Romans that we met with in our reflection on Paul had carried over into the fourth century Church, at least among the Roman elite. There was now a considerable overlap between Christians and pagans, many of whom were in fact monotheists and worshipped their own single deity. Boundaries were unclear. It is unlikely someone as perceptive as Augustine would have been unaware of this unwelcome fluidity.

As a result of the invasion of Rome by the heretical Alaric, large numbers of Catholic Christians were fleeing south into North Africa bringing pluralistic attitudes with them. It was chaos, just what Augustine hated. It was like being at sea again. What he craved was stability: solid ground.

By now a bishop, his reaction was to impose strict discipline and order, and to adopt a hard line on matters of morality and theology. His policy was, as he put it, 'to strive with the sword of God's word to free others from the grip of sin', regardless of whether that sin was theological or sexual. And, if people didn't agree with him, they must be compelled to do so.

It was a command and control strategy that led to an equivalent command and control theology that has echoed disastrously down the ages, through internecine religious conflict. Of course, the 'command' concept was very familiar to the early Christians. The Ten 'Commandments' of the Old Testament appear to be just that: commands. But are they?

Stay with that word for a moment. Did Jesus order people about? Did he try to control people? He worked hard to inspire and convince them, but not force them into submission. He left the choice to the other person who was free to walk away. While he spoke with authority, it was always matched by an engaging courtesy.

Jesus points out the way the rich are damaging the poor, but the word command is seldom on his lips, apart from when he quotes the Old Testament 'commandment' to love God and our neighbour or when he is commanding supposed evil spirits to leave their victims in the healing miracles.

But, if Jesus doesn't impose or 'command' obedience, does God? If Jesus is the human expression of the nature of God, then that means God is like Jesus. So does God really 'command' us to love each other? It is certainly possible: you can be commanded to work in ways that bring about the well-being and fulfilment of another person. God can say: whether you like the other person or not, you are commanded to treat them in a life-giving way. And that command could be backed up with the threat of punishment for non-compliance. But that seems to go against the essential nature of love.

Strange as it may sound, the so-called Ten Commandments could be interpreted as expressions of liberation, and therefore of love. Perhaps the stern 'thou shalt not' prefix was simply a way of guiding people away from the life-denying entanglements of temptation and self-destruction.

Seen in this light, the first commandment that 'You shall have no other gods before/beside me' (Deuteronomy 5:7) isn't an expression of latent jealousy but a way of urging us to stay true to life and freedom. Perhaps, above all, not to worship the god of money. You can't serve both God and mammon, Jesus warns in Luke 16:13. Similarly, 'Do not covet' is a plea not to become addicted to or imprisoned by possessions – and thereby lose sight of life's real gift, as the rich young man had done.

If we can see the 'commandments' as expressions of love we realise they sound much more like entreaties than commands backed up by threats. However, conditioned by centuries of tradition to think of commands in terms of imperial orders, it must have been difficult for people to imagine how there could be an all-powerful God who does not issue commands. And it still is. So maybe there's something not quite right with our view of God?

Womanly images

In the past, when people spoke about God, they naturally tended to use images that reflected contemporary thinking. They were images of masculinity because, in the world, they saw political authority expressed by men. In particular, kings who wielded enormous power. But, as we have discovered, that imagery is in conflict with the picture of God that Jesus shows us.

The crowd listening to him expected the father in the story of the prodigal son to be fearsome and manly, but he wasn't. He was behaving more like a typical mother in his willingness to put love before dignity. His response to the son was powerful, as womanliness frequently is, but it was not vengeful. Similarly, in the Lord's Prayer, the Abba word for 'father' expresses the warmth and love that we often associate with womanliness. A word of nurture. A word that gives birth to life. A word of mutuality. A word of resurrection.

The Church, however, has been drawn to hierarchical male imagery. St Luke (11:2) simply has the words 'Father, hallowed be your name . . .', but the Church prefers St Matthew's 'Our Father who art in heaven (6:9) which, instead, introduces a sense of formality and distance. Then, following an unknown source, the Church often adds: 'For yours is the kingdom, the power and the glory.'

In contrast, the Jesus word 'Abba' expresses intimacy, and therefore vulnerability, which is in stark contrast to the image of a warrior king sitting enthroned on high in power and glory. It is a word that speaks not with the voice of thunder, whirlwind and fire, but with the still small voice. In first-century Palestine, Jesus was that voice.

Instead of acting like a king who might build a fortress from which to impose his will, Jesus chose to live an itinerant ministry of servanthood and poverty. The fact that he was always on the move was partly about spreading a vision of hope among the scattered rural poor, but it also expressed the nature of the dynamic God of the Way.

Earthly kings, however, want their thrones to be secure. Fixed. Static. Similarly with their palaces. Yet fortresses and palaces, regarded by the world as signs of strength, are often symptoms of fear and weakness. And this is reflected in our own situation today.

Wealth and power can be signs of insecurity. The rich guard their possessions because they fear someone will take those possessions away. Just as they themselves have taken from the poor. But possessions also affect how we relate to others. We are increasingly realising that the more we love possessions, the less likely we are to love people. The more materialistic we get, the worse it seems is our relationship with others – and with the planet.

And the Church is not exempt from this. We seem fixated on expressions of power and numerical success by struggling to fill our churches and cathedrals with worshippers. But what is a cathedral? It may be a finite expression of our desire to give glory to God, or it can be an expression of status and power. A political statement.

When William the Conqueror invaded England in 1066 he set about mercilessly imposing Norman rule on the existing Anglo-Saxon culture. To this end he built mighty castles across the land. And equally impressive stone cathedrals, often on the sites of wooden Anglo-Saxon churches. He was intent on obliterating the past and stamping his rule on the entire country. His Norman churches and cathedrals were not just places of worship, they were statements of power and long-term possession.

Those Christian invaders had obviously forgotten the Old Testament portrayal of God as one who warns *against* erecting fine buildings (Jeremiah 35:7) and who abhors carved masonry. Majestic buildings give many people a sense of security, an emotional refuge.

The trouble is that the more we put our trust in bricks and mortar, the more we are in danger of denying God's love for us.

But we like the security of imposing buildings. They become an emotional refuge. It was rather like that with the disciples. Out on the Sea of Galilee, Jesus told Peter to get out of the boat and come to him. But, as we know, Peter wanted to stay in the boat where it was safe. At that moment, that boat was his castle.

A hand cart to hell?

In some ways the Church has chosen to follow Peter, rather than risk the Jesus option. It has presented itself as the 'ship' of salvation on the turbulent waters of the world. Jesus challenges us to take up our cross and follow him into uncertainty and danger, but the Church gravitates towards security and orderliness where its power can be defended.

One of the ways it has defended its power has been to discourage its members from rocking the boat. It has done that by an increasingly complex theological control mechanism, ultimately involving the threat of excommunication and the prospect of hell as a punishment for non-compliance.

As we have seen, there are hints of this control in the Genesis story of Adam and Eve. God tells Adam that, because he has listened to his wife, both he and Eve and all future generations of humanity will be cursed. Expelled from the Garden of Eden into a harsh world outside. Out of the garden of paradise into eternal desolation. Message: that's what you get for not doing as you're told.

Surprisingly, however, belief in hell had not historically been part of Hebrew thinking. There was the belief that, after death, you descended into Sheol: a shadowy place of forgetfulness, but you didn't cease to exist. The idea of hell as a place of punishment and suffering came from the Greeks in the fourth century BCE, after the conquest of Alexander the Great.

But by the Middle Ages, the idea of hell was reaching maximum velocity, helped by writers like Dante with his horrifying images of eternal suffering in *The Inferno,* and the spread of the Black Death across Europe.

However, there was more to come. Christians believed that only faith could save them from eternal damnation but with the Protestant theologian John Calvin, came the surreal idea that whether you were ultimately saved or damned had been already preordained by God – before you were even born.

Today in the twenty-first century, many Christians in the western Church still believe in hell as a real place or, at least, as a real consequence of sin. Those who hold to traditional church teaching believe they are saved by the cross of Jesus. But saved from what? The anger of God?

In that case, what sort of God are we talking about? A vindictive God, full of wrath, willing to punish and torment humanity for their mistakes for all eternity? A God who inflicts the most disproportionate revenge on the human race for a single act of disobedience by one person?

You might think we have left all that behind in the Old Testament. But, as we have hinted earlier, it resurfaces in Matthew's Gospel. In Matthew chapter 25, we are presented with almost a mirror of the Genesis story. And, like the story of the Garden of Eden, it paints a grotesque picture of God. It describes a king (Jesus) on a royal throne, separating his subjects into sheep and goats. The sheep are the ones who responded to need with kindness: the goats are those who withheld even a cup of water. The good sheep are welcomed into the king's reward but the goats are condemned to eternal suffering.

As a story it is certainly memorable, but theologically it's hideous. Firstly, the idea of Jesus sitting in glory is imagery from long after the resurrection. The last thing the earthly Jesus would want to do was to sit on a throne. Out in the wilderness, the Devil had already tempted him with that idea and it didn't work. A throne symbolises hierarchy. It's about power directed at people of lower status. For the whole of his ministry Jesus opposed exactly that dynamic.

Secondly, Jesus did not do separation. Separation excludes but Jesus was radically inclusive. Even the enemy was welcomed with a loving embrace when the rich young man came asking for guidance.

Thirdly, as we have seen, Jesus used characteristically brief sayings when he taught. But the sheep and goats story is a yard long. We have also noticed that when a long 'Jesus' story comes in two halves, it is worth questioning the authenticity of the second part.

And, in this case, it's the second part that presents the problem.

Fourthly, the story says that, for the sake of a single moment of neglect, withholding a cup of water, we bring down on ourselves eternal damnation. The wrath of God. What sort of God is that? A static, robotic God programmed to react with violence at the slightest hint of human frailty? A cruel tyrant, likely to respond to the merest fault with unspeakable fury?

So what is going on? Think back to Mark 9:41, which was probably written 20 or 30 years earlier than Matthew. Here Jesus says that anyone who gives one of his thirsty followers a drink of water will be blessed. End of statement: no hint of negativity. It is quite possible that Matthew took Mark's simple sentence and improved on it – with disastrous results.

Does it matter? It matters massively. The sheep and goats story is like the Exodus narrative: it involves separation and condemnation. And like the Exodus story, it is memorable. Even in today's secular world, the phrase 'the sheep and the goats' is instantly recognised as dividing the supposedly good from the bad. The noble from the ignoble; the rich from the poor; the powerful from the powerless. The Christian from the unbeliever.

In that separation lurks oppression, injustice and genocide. And, as we are discovering, when it comes to separation from the planet and our living environment, something immeasurably worse.

As in the story of Adam and Eve, the transgression described is individual. The sin is one of personal disobedience to the will of God. The result of both narratives is to focus down on the individual sinner.

Jesus, however, shows remarkably little interest in personal sins. As we saw, he did not even bother to ask what sins the paralysed man on the stretcher might have committed, before assuring him of forgiveness. Jesus was concerned about structural sin. The systematic oppression of the poor by the rich; stigmatising those who were vulnerable; the marginalisation of women by men.

Choosing to follow the individualistic mindset of St Matthew's story, the Church has repeatedly ignored the structural injustice that Jesus opposed – and which led to the cross. The God that Jesus embodies and proclaims has a sorrow or even an anger at injustice, but it is simply impossible for such a God to be consistent with, or the creator of, hell. There cannot be God and hell. The two are mutually exclusive.

This view is held by many in the Eastern Orthodox Church who are appalled by what they see as the punitive and destructive theology of the Augustinian West. While the western Church has focused on the transactional 'saving' nature of Christ's death on the cross, they have seen the love-in-action Incarnation as the crucial event. And so it is.

A godless Church?

At the end of the day, all that matters is God. If there is no God then life has no meaning and human actions have no value other than those we arbitrarily choose to invent. If there is no God, then we are little more than random organisms clinging to the surface of a small piece of rock flying through an apparently dead universe.

But over the millennia, rightly or wrongly, many people have come to believe there is an external creative force giving life and value to existence. From Africa, the cradle of humanity, and the Middle East has emerged a belief in something we call God. Then, through Judaism in particular, came the idea that God is just and loving.

Christians believe that, as humanity drew gradually closer to this awareness of God, it was as though there was a spark. A moment of ignition. One day, in around 4CE in a small country of no apparent consequence, the nature of God was expressed in a human being.

The Church calls this the Incarnation. It holds that event to be of infinite importance, even though it doesn't always seem to believe it to be true. But why might the Church not believe the Incarnation to be true? Because the Church, it appears, doesn't believe in God. That sounds so ridiculous, it needs some unpacking.

The Church certainly believes in the idea of God, but it seems to have great difficulty accepting the *reality* of God. If Jesus is the human expression of God, he shows us that the fundamental characteristic of God's nature is love. Outgoing love expressed as justice and compassion. Jesus, who the Church believes is God in human form, gave his life for that reality. It was central to his existence.

The institutional Church, however, has largely avoided, ignored and obscured that reality. Trapped within its own hierarchical structures and protective dogmas, it has been afraid to live the life Jesus shows us. But if the Church believes that God holds all life in being, why should it be afraid of anything?

In the past, and still today, politicians and others in power have subjected tens of millions of vulnerable people to appalling suffering and death. Despite the clear gospel imperative to love our neighbour and give justice to the poor, the Church has repeatedly colluded with that injustice. It has been silent in the face of suffering, and walked past on the other side.

Some, like Archbishop Oscar Romero, have given their lives willingly in the struggle for God's compassionate justice for the poor. Others, women and men, Christian and non-Christian, have done the same. But the vast majority of those in the Church have not done so. And their compliant silence has been an effective endorsement of injustice.

Why would a Church that claims a profound belief in a loving and all-powerful God fear criticism and death? If we truly believe in God, then death holds no terrors. But the institutional Church shows every sign of alarm and consternation at even the suggestion of disapproval by politicians and a hostile press.

We might therefore be forgiven for assuming that the Church does not actually believe in the reality of the God, whom it proclaims. Nor is it really committed to follow the one it says is the incarnation of that loving

God. Instead it imprisons the turbulent radical Jesus in the soundproof padded cell of institutional religion. And the consequences of that may very soon be catastrophic for us all.

13

Postscript:
Staring into the abyss

We began this book by recognising that the survival of the human race is threatened by the impending disaster of climate change. We suggested the Church could play a pivotal role in averting that catastrophe, but only if it radically changes its attitude to the world and recalibrates some of its most basic beliefs. To do that, we argued, it would need to rediscover the real Jesus of the Gospels.

Assisted by the onion diagram and many gifted writers who have gone before us, we explored the political and economic situation against which Jesus spoke out. We saw how he challenged the oppression inflicted by the Roman Empire on the poor and marginalised. How his seemingly gentle stories were often powerful expressions of outrage at injustice and greed.

Now, at the end of this book, we need to take a long hard look at ourselves. In some ways our world mirrors that of first-century Palestine. A rich and powerful elite control most of the world's resources and wealth. As a result millions are condemned to live and die in poverty.

In the rich West the poor are stigmatised as worthless scroungers by politicians and a media controlled by wealthy vested interests. Not long ago research found that most churchgoers in the UK actually thought the current harsh benefits regime was too generous.

In the time of Jesus the religious system created a similar hostility towards the poor who were often condemned as unclean and sinful. If Jesus was angry at those injustices, he must be outraged by the way the poor and vulnerable are treated today. Churches frequently hand out food to the poor but seldom demand to know why the poor have no food. It is as though they have bought into St Paul's belief that those in power are appointed by God to maintain social order and that religion should not meddle in politics.

Nor is this a new development. Back in the nineteenth century Charles Dickens was furious at his local vicar and others like him who organised food handouts to the poor while ignoring the systemic injustice causing the poverty in the first place.

That silent complicity continues to serve the interests of the rich today. But, as we have realised, there is one huge difference between our world and that of Dickens. Not only do the poor suffer exploitation and injustice, the whole human race is confronted by the possibility of its own destruction. The latest scientific prediction is that we have only a few years left. After that it will be too late. We are staring into the abyss.

In the face of this nightmare, does it matter what the Church believes? Most people might say that it doesn't. However, the world has reached the point where, unexpectedly, it might matter a great deal. If the

Church took the reality of the radical Jesus seriously, the two billion people who self-identify as Christian could make a crucial difference to the climate change crisis. Add to that four billion people of other faiths, most of which teach respect for their neighbour – and therefore the planet.

Acting collaboratively alongside atheist and agnostic humanists, they could influence governments and international corporations. Working together for the good of all humanity we could exert massive influence and political leverage.

Who might oppose such dramatic and controversial action? The answer has already been identified: vested interests. Multi-national corporations are some of our worst polluters. Wielding enormous influence over politicians and committed to maximising profits, they are not going to surrender their power and wealth without a fight.

A grieving God

Jesus was strongly opposed to hierarchical power systems controlled by men and the corresponding injustice inflicted on women. Is it a coincidence that today's powerful capitalist corporations have arisen in a male-dominated competitive market? What might happen if those words – competitive, dominated and male – were replaced with three different words: collaborative, cooperative and female?

It is not enough to halt climate change. We also need to find a different, less destructive way of conducting human affairs. Is it naive to suggest that women could play a key role, not only in averting climate disaster but also in building a more sustainable future for us all? Women as young as the teenage Mary Magdalene or Greta Thunberg.

For centuries, in the Church and in the world, arrogant, competitive men have held positions of leadership. They are the reason we are in such a dangerous situation today. We need women to inject thoughtful, strategic rationality into the human race.

For the first time in history we have the power to destroy our own species and the vast numbers of other life forms that make up our living environment. We have the knowledge to travel to other planets but do not have the wisdom to preserve our own planetary life support system. I, like many others, will not live to see the full impact of that suicidal process of greed and exploitation, but our children and grandchildren will. What will they think of us as life around them disintegrates?

Despite all the opportunities that knowledge and intelligence have given us, we will have poisoned our beautiful planet and destroyed its fragile, life-giving ecology. What a tragic legacy after millions of years of human evolution. A polluted planet journeying for all eternity through a silent universe. And a grieving God whose only desire is that we should have life in its fullness, and whose love is poured out for us all.

Approximate
Time Line

Approximate Time Line

(CE = Common Era)

700BCE	Greek writer Hesiod creates story of Pandora
550BCE	Babylonian exile of Hebrews. Genesis probably written
332BCE	Alexander the Great invades Palestine
63BCE	Romans conquer Jerusalem
50BCE	Democracy in Rome replaced by dictatorship
44BCE	Julius Caesar assassinated. Period of instability
31BCE	Augustus becomes dictator. Period of stability
04CE	Birth of Jesus
14CE	Augustus dies. Succeeded by Tiberius
30CE	Jesus begins his public ministry

30CE	Political turmoil in Rome
33CE	Jesus executed by Romans
37CE	Tiberius dies
45CE +	Paul travelling, writing his letters
55CE+	Mark gathering material for his Gospel
55CE	Paul executed by the Romans
63CE+	Mark writing his Gospel
65CE	Mark's Gospel completed
70CE	Jerusalem Temple destroyed by Romans
75CE+	Matthew and Luke's Gospels written
100CE+	John's Gospel written

Acknowledgements and Thanks

Contributions to the thinking behind this book have come from a large number of sources, both formal and informal. The following are remembered with gratitude and admiration, others forgotten with embarrassment. None has been knowingly quoted: all would provide valuable further reading:

Beard, Mary: *SPQR* (Profile Books, 2016)

Biko, Steve: *I Write What I Like* (Penguin, 1988)

Bonhoeffer, Dietrich: *Letters and Papers from Prison* (Fontana, 1966)

Borg, Marcus: *Jesus* (Harper One, 2006)

Borg, Marcus and Crossan, John Dominic: *The First Paul* (Harper One, 2009)

Borg, Marcus and Crossan, John Dominic: *The Last Week* (SPCK, 2008)

Crossan, John Dominic: *Jesus, a Revolutionary Biography* (Harper Collins, 1994)

Crossan, John Dominic: *The Historical Jesus* (Harper One, 1992)

Hanson, K.C. and Oakman, Douglas: *Palestine in the Time of Jesus* (Fortress, 1998)

Herzog, William: *Parables as Subversive Speech* (Westminster/John Knox, 1994)

Hooper, Keith: *Charles Dickens: Faith, Angels and the Poor* (Lion Hudson, 2017)

Hoppe, Leslie: *There Shall Be No More Poor Among You* (Abingdon, 2004)

Kalomiros, Alexandre: *The River of Fire* (St Nectarios Press, 1980)

Murry, J. Middleton: *The Betrayal of Christ by the Churches* (Andrew Dakers, 1940)

Myers, Ched*: Binding the Strong Man* (Orbis, 2006)

Pagola, Jose: *Jesus: an Historical Approximation* (Convivium, 2013)

Pope Francis: *Laudato Si* (St Paul's Publishing, 2015)

Tolstoy, Leo: *The Gospel in Brief* (Dover Publications, 2008)

Wills, Gary: *What Paul Meant* (Penguin, 2006)

Other books by David Rhodes on social justice and spirituality include: *Faith in Dark Places, The Advent Adventure, Lenten Adventure, Sparrow Story*, and *Finding Mr Goldman.* All available online.